The Welcoming
Garden

The Welcoming Garden

Designing Your Own Front Garden

GORDON HAYWARD

Gibbs Smith, Publisher
Salt Lake City

First Edition
10 09 08 07 06   5 4 3 2 1

Text © 2006 Gordon Hayward
Illustrations © 2006 Elayne Sears
Photographs © 2006 as noted

Published by
Gibbs Smith, Publisher
P.O. Box 667
Layton, Utah 84041

Orders: 1.800.748.5439
www.gibbs-smith.com

Designed by Steve Rachwal
Printed and bound in Hong Kong

Library of Congress Cataloging-in-
Publication Data
Hayward, Gordon.
The welcoming garden : designing your own
front garden / Gordon Hayward.— 1st ed.
   p. cm.
ISBN 1-58685-704-5
1. Landscape gardening. I. Title.

SB473.H392 2005
635.9—dc22

2005012298

PHOTOGRAPHY CREDITS

Anita Bracalente: 2.1, 8.4

Karen Bussolini: 2.9, 4.7, 4.8, 5.2, 5.8, 6.3, 6.5, 8.3, 10.5, 10.6, 10.7, A (page 32)

Robin Cushman: 2.6, 4.1, 5.1, 5.6, 7.1, 8.1, 10.1, 10.2, 10.3, 10.4, 10.8, 10.9, 10.10, 10.11

John Glover: D (page 66)

Saxon Holt: 1.4, 2.3, 2.7, 2.8, 3.1, 4.3, 4.4, 4.5, 5.4, 5.5, 6.2, 6.4, 7.4, 9.1, 9.2

Jerry Howard: 6.1

Irene Jeruss: 1.5, 2.2, 3.5, 3.6

Andrea Jones: 2.5, 8.5, C (page 54)

Dency Kane: 4.6, 5.3, 7.2, 8.2, B (page 54)

Jerry Pavia: 1.1, 1.2, 2.4, 3.2, 3.3, 3.4, 4.2, 7.3, 7.5, 8.6, E (page 123)

Pam Spaulding: 1.3, 5.7

To all the garden photographers whose images made this,

and all my books, come alive with color and clarity.

Contents

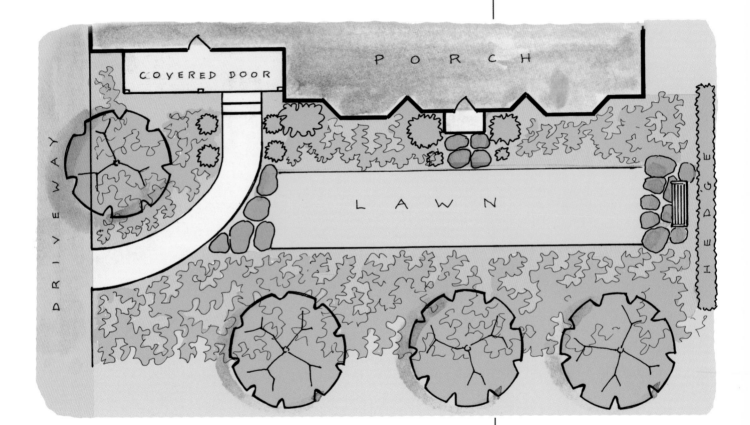

Acknowledgments

AFTER I GAVE a garden design lecture in June 2003 at The Utah Museum of Fine Arts in Salt Lake City, publisher Gibbs Smith came up to me and said he felt we could work well together. I was flattered by his faith in me on the strength of an hour's lecture; after subsequent meetings in his offices in a barn in rural Utah, we began our collaboration.

I contacted my agent, Christina Ward, so that she could get the ball rolling. Gibbs Smith asked editor Hollie Keith to work with me. As the weeks and months passed, I wrote to many photographers asking for images they had taken of gardens at the front of houses across America. Nearly two thousand slides arrived from them: Karen Bussolini and Irene Jeruss in Connecticut; Robin Cushman in Eugene, Oregon; Saxon Holt in California; Andrea Jones in England; Dency Kane in New York City; Jerry Pavia in Idaho; as well as Pat Bruno of Positive Images, who represents photographers Pam Spaulding, Jerry Howard and John Glover.

As our garden in Vermont was under a blanket of snow during the winter of 2004, I spent many happy hours studying slides of remarkable gardens designed by home gardeners and professional designers from across America and Canada. I selected those you see in this book.

In the meantime I gained permission from nearly thirty clients for whom I have designed entry gardens over the years to have schematic drawings done of their gardens. With their kind permission and nearly thirty blueprints in hand, I met over the kitchen table with illustrator Elayne Sears at her home in New York State. She subsequently created all the drawings you see here.

I want to sincerely thank all of these people for their good work, their easy cooperation, and their faith in my work as a writer and designer.

The foundation on which this and all my other books and articles are built was created over twenty-five years of fruitful collaboration with many people: John Barstow, now of Chelsea Green Press in Vermont; Roger Swain and Nan Sinton of *Horticulture Magazine*; Tom Cooper; and Todd Meier and Virginia Small of *Fine Gardening Magazine.* My heartfelt thanks go out to all of you.

I would also like to thank my parents, John and Helen Hayward, who taught me how to be welcoming, for they were themselves possessed of open hearts.

And finally, I would like to thank my dear wife, Mary, for everything she has given me under the sun, the moon and the sky.

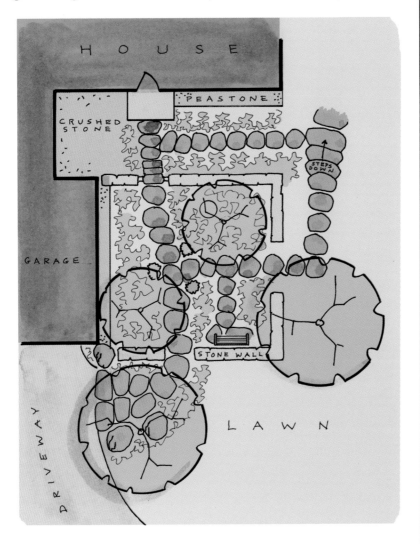

Introduction

THERE IS A LOT OF TALK among gardeners across North America about rethinking our front gardens. Google "front garden" on the Internet and up will come thousands of entries. There are competitions in rural towns, suburban neighborhoods and gated communities for the best front garden. There are Web sites from individuals who have remade their entry gardens, are proud of what they've accomplished and want the world to know. There are even Web sites put up by people who live in apartment buildings who have formed gardening committees to transform battered lawns at the front of their multistory buildings into richly planted vegetable or flower gardens.

The editors of national gardening magazines know how compelling the front garden is too. Look into nearly every issue of *Horticulture Magazine* or *Fine Gardening Magazine* and you will find an article about an entry garden. Look at books like this one and you will see how front gardens welcome, enliven, enrich and engage us, while foundation planting leaves us cold. Front gardens make our homes feel cozy and enclosed. Good front gardens send us off to work in the morning, welcome us home in the evening and engage us every weekend; and, because they are out front, neighbors and passersby get pulled into the mix too.

Will and Sara Anne Godwin live in a suburb outside Hagerstown, Maryland. I worked with them a few years back to create an easily manageable garden in an eighteen-foot-deep, forty-foot-long garden space at the front of their house. It's basically a central panel of lawn surrounded by trees, flowering shrubs and perennials right out to the sidewalk. They tell me they sit on their front porch most evenings during the growing season and, invariably, neighbors out for an evening stroll stop to chat about the garden. The Godwins also see neighbors taking their first tentative steps toward redefining their own front gardens.

In Utah, gardeners are planting a row of crab apple trees out by the sidewalk to make the front lawn more private. In Oregon, they're taking up all the lawn between house and sidewalk, planting cherry trees in the resulting garden space, and then underplanting them with a richly diverse collection of shrubs and low-maintenance perennials, as you'll see in chapter 10. In Arizona, gardeners are not putting any lawn out front; they're creating spare and startling gardens with plants native to the Southwest. Foundation planting—that cliché that means glomming a few evergreen shrubs against the front foundation of the house and then running lawn from it down to the sidewalk or street—is becoming a thing of the past.

The new American garden means living and walking among plants, following a path from driveway to front door among ornamental grasses and Russian sage, talking with friends under apple and cherry trees at the front of the house. The new American front garden is embodied in what Carol and Jim Farnes have created in Corvallis, Oregon: a garden for themselves that they openly share with their neighbors. Walk along the sidewalk in their suburban community and you'll come upon a gate into their entry garden with a sign that reads, "Welcome to the garden. Please come in."

A Step-By-Step Approach

To help you make your own front garden more personal, engaging and private, I have organized this book following the step-by-step process I and other design professionals follow when designing entry gardens. I start by helping you determine the overarching priority—the Big Idea—that will help you make all the smaller decisions. A shady front lawn can suggest a woodsy garden with no lawn; a formal house might call for formal beds and lawns in geometric shapes. Once you have an overarching idea for your entry garden, the first step is to decide where the path will go from where you and/or your guests park your car and walk to the front door. That path not only breaks up the big design idea into at least two parts, but its beginning and end also provide clues as to where trees go, what shrubs might go under those trees, and what perennials and small shrubs might go in along the path. Those decisions will, in turn, help you decide how much lawn to leave or remove, or where to place ornaments, planted pots and maybe even window boxes.

The purpose of this book is not to overwhelm you with more garden than you can manage. Its purpose is to help you find your level of comfort and confidence, to help you see how you can make those first steps to redefine your front garden in a way that is comfortable and manageable.

Because the focus of this book is *your* front garden, as you read the book and study the photographs, keep the space at the front of your house foremost in your mind. Furthermore, be nonjudgmental as you look at various photos. The point is not whether you like the garden pictured—we all have differing tastes—but what you can learn from the image that you can realistically apply to your own developing front garden. Once you clearly understand design principles, which are guidelines for action, you can then go to work in your front garden with confidence and a plan you can develop comfortably over time.

How to Look at Photos of Gardens

To get to that point of confidence, however, you need to know how to look at pictures of gardens in books like this one so you can fully understand the principles they are meant to illustrate. My job is to show you the design principles in each photo. Your job is to apply them to the area at the front of your house so you can see what to do first, second, third. . . . Engage your imagination; attend to the images; give them time to work their magic on you. Out of the nearly two thousand slides I considered, I have chosen about seventy-five to help illustrate useful design principles that you can put to work in your own garden, no matter what size, no matter where it is in North America. As a garden writer, I hope to help you see those principles in these seventy-five images, and I want to help you apply those principles in a way that feels fresh and right for you in light of your budget, your skills and the amount of time you have to give to the project.

To help you know how to look at these images—as well as photos in all those other gardening books you own—let's look at a photo of a front garden in California that appears here as well as in chapter 7 (figure 7.3) as an example. First of all, don't look at the photo and think, "I don't live in California; maybe the next picture will show a house in Michigan where I live." Don't think, "I don't want a fence out by my sidewalk," and turn the page. Do think, "Here's a house not far from a sidewalk. Let's see how they handled the space to see if it has any lessons for me." Work with the image; think about it; take several minutes with it until you see its relevance to your entry garden.

Here are some questions to ask about this photo, the answers to

FIGURE 7.3 *No matter where you live, every photograph in this book is rich with ideas for your garden once you learn how to interpret garden photographs. Spend time thinking about these images and you'll teach yourself a great deal about garden design.*

which might prove useful as you think about your own front garden:

- *Should I install some kind of fence out by the sidewalk or street to separate the public walkway from my private front garden? If so, should I make a fence like the one in the picture or would I prefer picket, split rail, stone or perhaps a hedge?*

- *If I do decide on a painted wooden fence, should I paint my fence the same color I painted my house to create a visual link between the two? How would it look if I painted it a different color?*

- *Should I leave a foot or more between sidewalk and fence for a strip of garden?*

- *Should I plant trees between my fence and the front of the house to create more separation between street and house and to soften the expanse of shingle on the roof?*

- *If so, what shrubs could I plant under those trees so I don't completely block the view from my living room window out to the street? Or do I want to obscure that view so when I'm in my front yard, I feel total privacy?*

- *What perennials could I plant under the shrubs to provide color and fragrance?*

- *Do I need some built structure over the landing by my front door to make the space feel more intimate? What vines could I grow up the supports of my front door arbor?*

- *There is a fence on the left side of the photo that appears to be running along the side of the driveway, thereby separating driveway from front garden. How could I separate my driveway from entry garden? With a fence? Hedge? A shrub border?*

- *Should I plant the strip of ground between my sidewalk and street as they have done in this picture?*

Start small and build on your success. You'll be surprised at how the spirit of your lively, engaging front garden will ripple out with encouragement across your neighborhood.

GARAGE

H O U S E

P O R C H

HERBS

B L U E S T O N E

PARKING

LAWN

EXISTING
WOODS

Chapter 1
The Style of Your Front Garden

CREATING HARMONY between your front garden and the front of your house is simply a matter of looking both outward and inward. To create that harmony, reacquaint yourself with the nature of your house. Take a look inside both it and yourself to see what characteristics they reflect.

Start with the house. Go outside and stand on the road, street or sidewalk and take a close look at the front of your house. Is it one, two or three stories high? When was it built? Does it have a certain style? Colonial? Victorian? Cottage? Arts and Crafts? Is it a ranch house or a classic suburban home with white clapboards? What materials were used in its construction? What color is the house and is that color different from the trim? What color is the front door? Is your house like most on your street or road, or does it have a distinctive style? Also look at existing features in the landscape, taking note of those elements that you cannot or do not want to change such as major trees, your home's proximity to the sidewalk or street, a garage or outbuildings.

Answers to these and other questions about your house will help you choose a style for the garden in front of it. A cottage-type house gives rise to a warm, informal garden. A distinctively painted house gives rise to a very colorful (or subdued) garden. A long, low house suggests a long, low garden. A rustic house in a rural area gives rise to a relaxed garden.

To further help describe the style of your front garden, think of it as an extension of the interior of your home. Over the years, as you chose furniture, objects for the walls, carpets for the floor and lamps for the tables, a style began to emerge. Take stock of that style. To help you see what I mean by a style shared between house and garden,

FIGURE 1.1 *The Freymiller garden in Solano Beach, California, punctuated by the white-blooming* Solanum jasminoides *over the front door, is a welcoming interplay of evergreen lawn and foliage against a white house with creamy yellow trim.*

turn through the pages of this book for a few moments to see how house and garden work together to create a unified whole.

Now think about yourself, because you have already made many choices about the style of your house and furnishings in light of your personality and the way you like to live. A better understanding of yourself will help you articulate the desired nature of your entry garden. Are you a formal person who enjoys clean edges, a tidy look and everything in its place? Or are you casual, exuberant or rambunctious? Are you spiritual? A vegetable gardener? A minimalist? Private or gregarious? What kinds of gardens have moved you?

Because the front garden and the façade of your house show your private face to public view, you also need to assess your relationship to your neighbors. What you do in your front garden has a lot to do with the nature of your relationship to them. You have to be clear how you want to proceed, because more often than not, your neighbors have a lawn at the front of their house with two trees, a winding walkway to the front door between them and evergreens growing along the foundation. For you to go off in some totally different gardening direction at the front of your house takes a lot of self-assurance and sensitivity to the needs of others. But take heart from Will and Sara Anne Godwin from Hagerstown, Maryland. They found that when they made a garden that was right for them at the front of their house, neighbors came to visit and took ideas home with them.

In your search for an overall style—one that will show you what to plant as well as what not to plant—you also need to be clear about how you will use your front garden, because those uses have important implications for garden style. Do you have children who need some or all of the existing lawn out front, or are you a fanatic gardener with no children so all the lawn can be turned to garden? If you had a greater sense of privacy out front, would you be inclined to sit in your front garden? Are you on a busy street where children, dogs and cars are going by all day long so some degree of privacy along the sidewalk or street will need to be created, or do you live on a quiet country lane?

Finally, you need to find out what municipal rules and regulations are in place regarding front gardens. If you live in a rural area, there are likely none at all. If you live in a densely populated area on a corner lot, there may be all kinds of regulations regarding location and height of plants vis-à-vis sight lines from cars on the street.

To help you assess the nature of the front of your house and what implications it might have for your new front garden, thumb through the photos in this book. I have organized the pictures in each chapter from most formal to least formal. What I hope you will see as you look through the photographs is a harmony between house and front garden: formal house, formal garden; informal house, informal garden; colorful house, colorful garden; country house, country garden. Somewhere in the seventy-five or so images in this book you may find an entry garden that starts you on the path to choosing the style for your own entry garden. Let's take a look at some front gardens now, keeping in mind that no matter where you live, no matter what your house looks like, there are lessons for you in every picture.

Lots of Lawn; Symmetry by the Door

An Arts and Crafts home owned by Larry and Lani Freymiller of Solano Beach, California (figure 1.1), has deep roof overhangs that emphasize the sheltering nature of the architecture. Big windows downstairs frame big views into the entry garden, while the paned-glass windows upstairs create a cozy feeling of enclosure. The soft white paint and creamy yellow trim are calm and restrained; cedar shake shingles add warmth while the decorative spindles on the front door add charm and detail. Mature trees at the back of the Freymillers' house set the house into, rather than on, the landscape.

The garden answers the restrained house. The lawn, which acts as a setting for this home, sweeps up to shrubs that flirt with the notion of foundation planting. But there are many details that make this landscape a garden. There is the white-blooming *Solanum jasminoides* hanging over the front door that answers the white walls of the house. (Notice the Freymillers chose a vine, the flowers of which would repeat rather than contrast with existing paint colors.) There are also shrubs and trees across the front of the house that are laid out asymmetrically, thereby adding a level of informality.

Yet symmetry, which comes from similar windows on both sides of the centrally placed front door, tightens this front garden and adds to a firm structure provided in part by the straight tile path to the front door. Pairs of plants and man-made objects balance one another on both sides of the path: a pair of cast-stone urns atop formal pedestals; two cast-stone pots holding similarly shaped boxwoods; the matched pair of shorn topiaries, each held within matching picket fences. One object that relaxes this symmetry is the woven basket sitting on the front-door landing. Another relaxing note comes in the choice of different evergreen shrubs planted in front of the windows.

What you have to take into account as you develop the style of your entry garden is whether or not this mix of symmetry/asymmetry is right for you and your house. Does repetition of forms on each side of your front door with a lot of lawn running between sidewalk and front garden fit your style and the formality it implies? Or would you feel more comfortable with a less formal style?

The Naturalistic Garden

The Burgener entry garden in San Diego, California (figure 1.2), has no symmetry whatsoever. Even though designer Linda Chisari repeated boulders and certain plants on each side of the path, their effect is balance, not symmetry. This beige stucco house has no hint of formal layout, and yours may not either. In fact, the large windows, open entry area and covered overhang all bespeak owners who enjoy being outside, or at the very least who enjoy looking out into a garden through large panels of glass. The result is an entry garden that reflects the open architecture of the house. The path's curves, justified by large boulders near them, feel natural.

Boulders set here and there along the length of the entry garden also establish a naturalistic feeling within this lawnless garden. Informal grasses and native shrubs that do not call undue attention to themselves support this natural look, while at the same time separating the driveway to the right from the path to the front door.

Muted colors also tie house to garden. The beige color of the house generates the paint color of the wooden fence. Chisari echoes this beige color in the boulder's undertones as well as in the pebble-embedded walkway. She chose plants with gray and dark green foliage that will bloom in subdued colors. The gray stones that form the risers in the walkway pick up the gray tones of the column base.

And yet for all these details, for all the perennials and shrubs, the house remains visible through the semitransparent screen provided by the garden. The view out from the windows, the view in from the sidewalk, remains possible. This is a house in a garden, yet it is not visually separate from street or sidewalk. This semitransparent garden might be an appropriate model for you, even though your house color and style, as well as plant and materials choices, might be completely different.

FIGURE 1.3 *Owners Hugh and Hope Davis have developed a Colonial revival cottage garden around their early Colonial home in Massachusetts. They have created a home they call The Farmstead, with a garden and nursery that include, on other sides of the house, a kitchen garden, a small orchard, and herb and perennial gardens, all with plants associated with the 1700s.*

An Old Weathered House, A Cottage Garden

As you can see in figure 1.3, the overarching style for this entry garden comes directly from the nature of this historic clapboard house built in 1723. In 1969, owners Hugh and Hope Davis bought the historic centered-chimney saltbox house and moved it to its present site in Leverett, Massachusetts. That year they began the development of a Colonial-style garden that would harken back to the 1700s.

Everything about the design of this garden is about the past. The house with its wide-open windows recalls a time when grandma would put a pie hot out of the oven to cool on that same windowsill. The garden outside this home is just as timeless, just as relaxed, just as homey. Look closely and you'll see old-fashioned plants like bee balm and salvia, foxglove and bleeding heart, catmint and lily, and a red geranium in a pot hanging by the door, all visually held in place by a low, rustic, woven-branch fence of the sort the early colonists would have fashioned. House and garden are in complete harmony, and there is nothing modern or self-conscious reflected in the design.

But look closely and along the bottom of the image you'll see lawn, an element that would not have existed this way in 1723. Lawn in this entry garden runs out to the driveway. You could change all that at the front of your house by creating an old-fashioned garden that runs out to your street in front of your old-fashioned house, with no lawn whatsoever.

An Artistic Garden, an Artistic House

There's nothing old-fashioned about designer Suzanne Porter's garden that she created at the front of her home in Berkeley, California (figure 1.4). Porter's entry garden tells a lot about her sense of style. Here is an artist at work, and as with any work of art, all parts relate. The color of the house, and her obvious love of unusual plants, drives every decision, yet everything she chooses is managed by an overall concept. The dark terra-cotta-colored house provides a striking background for a garden based on color and texture.

FIGURE 1.4 *Designer Suzanne Porter planted the chartreuse-leaved* Phormium 'Yellow Wave' *to contrast with her rust-colored house; the evergreen tree* Camellia japonica *provides screening from a front window; the dwarf Japanese barberry (*Berberis thunbergii*) hedge at the front keeps dogs out yet echoes the undertones in the paint color of the house. The Azara tree provides frilly contrast.*

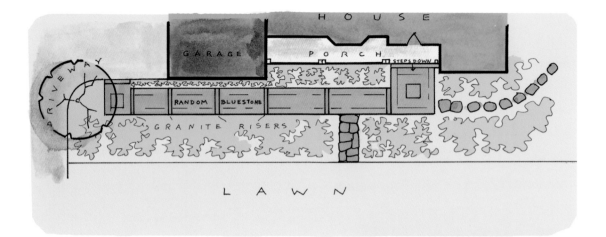

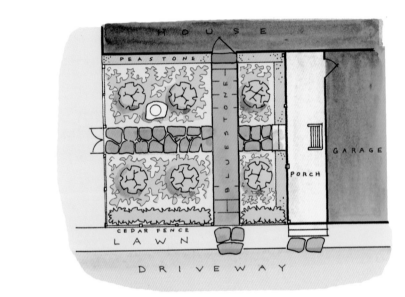

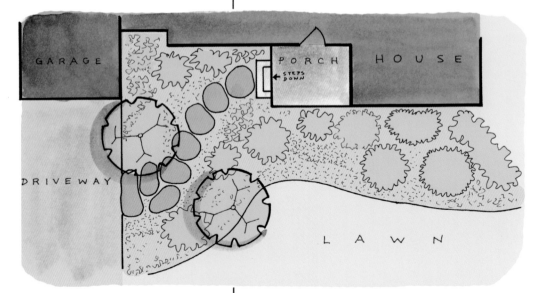

First, she planted three trees of contrasting leaf color and foliage type in order to set the house within a group of trees. Had she relied solely on low shrubs or perennials, the house would have appeared to be rising above the garden. By setting the house within the group of three different trees, something you could do, she creates a context, a place within which her house nestles.

To make sure the large window wouldn't become too distracting, she painted its trim dark green, a color that nearly matches the glossy green foliage of the *Camellia japonica* to the right of the picture. Next she created a low hedge out by the sidewalk with *Berberis thunbergii* 'Crimson Pygmy' (now a plant that is considered invasive) in part because some of the colors in the foliage echo the color of her house. In many ways the hedge and the house act as bookends that contain this garden.

Between those bookends she chose plants that light up in contrast to the color of the house or complement it. For example, she chose the white-blooming Autumn Moor Grass (*Sesleria autumnalis*) for both sides of the path to contrast with the house and Japanese Blood Grass (*Imperata cylindrica* 'Rubra') to echo the color of the house. Then, in a stroke of genius, she planted the massive variegated New Zealand Flax (*Phormium* 'Yellow Wave'), whose sword-shaped leaves absolutely shine against the rust-colored background of her house. She also chose an Azara tree just to the left of her window, the color of the trunk being virtually the same as the stone surrounds of the nearby window.

If you look closely at the cheek walls on each side of the steps up to her front door, you will see she has placed terra-cotta pots that are themselves very close in color to her house and then planted them with chocolate brown, rust-colored foliage plants accented with red-flowering and chartreuse-leaved plants. This is an artist who saw that the house itself could generate an all-encompassing style that would help her—and could help you—marry house to garden.

FIGURE 1.5 *This house in northwestern Connecticut is utterly surrounded by a garden. Jan Nickel is the owner and designer.*

The Green Dream

Jan Nickel, who lives and gardens in Avon, Connecticut, created her overarching idea not so much from the house as from the idea that she wanted to live in a house—its style is unimportant—completely surrounded by a lawless garden. She developed her garden design solely based on plants rather than plants in relation to the style of her house, and this may well be the right model for you. She calls her house and garden "Green Dreams." In surrounding her house with a garden of trees, shrubs, perennials and bulbs, something you could also do over time, she frees herself from having to find that balance between the architecture of her house and the layout of plants, lawn and hardscaping.

Look back for a moment and you'll see that the first garden in this chapter was generated by symmetry, the second by the nature of the architecture and its locale, the third by the historic qualities of the house, and the fourth by the color and style of the house. Here, Nickel offers another alternative to the Big Idea, one that is admittedly ambitious: live in a house totally surrounded by plants. Such a garden relies on subtle shades of foliage texture and color, of massing certain plants and highlighting single-specimen plants in other areas. For example, look closely at figure 1.5 and you'll see that Nickel placed a finely textured fern next to bold ligularia foliage so that one emphasizes the qualities of the other through pleasing contrast. She planted a variegated dogwood and then placed a uniformly green-leaved *Baptisia australis* next to it.

Now look at her front-door landing and you will see playful gatherings of artifacts, white columns, gray urns on gray pedestals and pineapple-shaped finials atop railing supports, all of which are laid out in an informal, easy way. These, as much as anything, set a lighthearted tone to this extensive entry garden.

Just imagine what it would be like to walk from window to window inside your house, looking into different parts of a garden that utterly surround your home. That is exactly what you could do (and what Nickel has done) if you are prepared over time to take up all that lawn and gradually surround your home with your own Green Dream so that you live in a house within a garden. Then imagine going out into that garden to walk among all those plants and see your house, whatever style it might be, nestled in a garden that runs across the entire front of your house and out to the street.

I can't tell you how many examples I have seen over the years of lawnless gardens that run from house to sidewalk. Whether in Ridgewood, New Jersey; Seattle, Washington; or San Francisco, California, they have one thing in common: the people who live in the houses surrounded by gardens are designers or passionate home gardeners who find great solace, pleasure and engagement in walking through a richly planted garden as they arrive home each day. They take all those same pleasures into the house, from which they look out into a garden that replenishes, enlivens and stimulates their lives every day of the year.

If your house and garden are drawn into a complementary visual and physical relationship with one another, your life will come into a new balance, a new yin-yang that balances inside and outside, plants and architecture, the man-made and the natural worlds.

DESIGN PRINCIPLES

- *An entry garden sets your house into the landscape, into a garden.*

- *The front of your house holds many cues as to the style of your new entry garden.*

- *The style of your house, its colors and materials, will hold clues for you when it comes to garden layout and plant choice.*

- *Straight paths feel more formal than curving paths.*

- *Symmetry leans toward formal; asymmetry leans toward casual.*

- *House color can visually link with the color of materials and plants to create a complementary relationship between house and garden.*

- *Materials in a small garden need to be limited to two or three so as not to create a busy, unsettled look.*

- *Fences can be used to create privacy as well as form a backdrop for a garden.*

- *Enclosing an entry garden with a fence, hedge or plantings out by the sidewalk increases the feeling of privacy.*

Chapter 2
Driveway, Cars and the Front Garden

ESTABLISHING THE OUTER PERIMETER of any garden is one of your first design steps. Get those edges right and you can see the limits of your design challenge. As you saw in chapter 1, the front of your house is the first and richest of those edges in that it provides so many design cues for your entry garden. The edge furthest from the front of your house may be the street, sidewalk or the limits you set on how far out your entry garden will go into your lawn. The edge at the far side of your entry garden may well be the boundary line between you and your neighbor where you might set a fence, wall, hedge or plantings.

The last edge is your driveway. It forms a straight or broadly curving line that is largely a given. It provides not only the fourth edge for your entry garden but also the starting point for the path that leads to your front door. That all-important path from driveway/parking to front door provides you with many of the cues you need to develop a coherent, welcoming entry garden.

Let's look at a variety of examples of how the driveway/parking can help develop many of the initial design ideas that, once made, can build your confidence as a designer. As always, keep the area at the front of *your* house foremost in mind as you read these examples.

Plant on Each Side of Your Driveway

As you can see in figure 2.1, the Marchants, who live in Indiana, have a driveway that runs straight along the front of their house to the garage. In many ways, the spine of their garden is the driveway itself, while the straight path from it to their front door is only a few feet long. Even though this long, narrow garden between front porch and driveway is very shallow, it makes all the difference. When sitting on

(FACING) FIGURE 2.1 Anita Bracalente, the designer of this garden in Indiana, saw the driveway as the spine of the garden. Even with the driveway so close to the front door and porch, family and guests feel they have arrived at a house in a garden.

the porch, the Marchants can look directly into this nearby flower border that answers the tasteful, restrained nature of the architecture. As they sit on this porch they surely feel they are in a garden.

But they didn't stop there. Their urge to garden leapt over the driveway to its other side. Rhododendrons, peonies and irises—all the colors of May—mean that the Marchants walk through a garden every time they come home and walk to the front door.

Now I'm going to add just a little aside here by way of reminding you not to be too literal when looking at figure 2.1 or any photograph in this book. The Marchant house may not be exactly like yours, but there are several universal design ideas here if you look creatively at this image:

> *Run the path straight out from the front door to a nearby driveway rather than curve or run it on a diagonal.*

> *Garden in the entire space between a nearby driveway and the front of your house.*

> *Plant low shrubs in that garden so when you sit in a rocking chair on the porch, the shrubs screen your view of the driveway but allow for a view of the garden across it.*

> *Let that same gardening style leap over your driveway so you drive through a garden every time you come home.*

FIGURE A *Photographer and garden designer Karen Bussolini designed this spring planting in a weather-proof polyethylene garland cylinder from Compania Pots. Because the pot isn't damaged by frost, Bussolini plants it with six different seasonal combinations, including one for winter. She places this pot at the bottom of the steps to her front door. The addition of the orange-tinged willow stems pushed lightly into the soil mix makes all the difference to this display of daffodils and primroses.*

POTS IN THE GARDEN

There are many appropriate places for planted pots in the garden: on the steps on either side of the front door; on either side of the beginning of the path into your front garden; next to a chair or bench; on a pedestal in the garden or where a path swells to go around a pot on a pedestal; at the junction of paths; massed on a broad landing by the front door. There are a number of images in this book that can be of further help. Refer to figures 1.3, 1.4, 4.1, 4.3, 4.7, 5.1, 5.4, 5.8, 6.1, 7.1, 8.2, 8.6, 10.1 and 10.7 for inspiration.

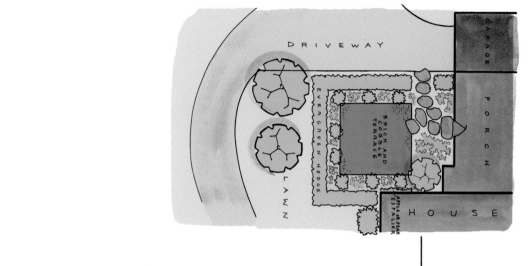

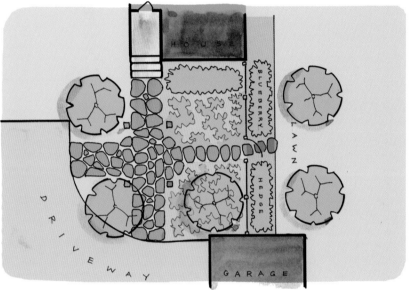

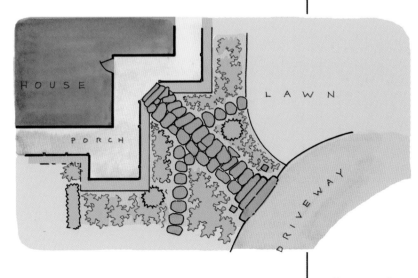

The Path between Parking Area and Front Door

Let's look back at Jan Nickel's garden to see what she has done to draw a line between parking area and front door. Figure 1.5 shows the garden gathered around Jan Nickel's front door; figure 2.2 steps back from that image to show you her whole front garden and how it relates to her parking/turnaround area. Nickel created a broad, beige-colored parking area for family and guests off her dark black macadam driveway. To show guests where to go once they get out of their car, she built a wooden walkway, punctuated by light-colored garden ornaments, to draw people to that first step. Once there, guests follow the curvilinear wooden walkway through her garden to arrive at the wooden landing by the front door. That curving wooden walkway shows off Nickel's entry garden by leading people directly through it.

But note: Nickel curved her walkway. Had she run it straight from parking to front door, people leaving the house would look down the length of the entry path to a framed view of cars sitting in the parking area. By curving her entry path, she is able to hide cars and driveway from many vantage points along all but the last few feet of the walkway as path approaches parking area. Stand by your front door and see if you can see parked cars and a lot of driveway. If you can, Jan Nickel's design might hold some lessons for you.

FIGURE 2.2 *Jan Nickel created a parking area within her front garden so guests can get out of their cars and step immediately into a garden. The path from parking area to front door curves, thereby building a mystery and an informality.*

Make a Small Entry Garden/Parking Area Feel Bigger

Suzanne Porter, whose entry garden you saw earlier in figure 1.4, doesn't have the luxury of all that space, as you can see in figure 2.3. She needs to park near the edge of her front garden, so the walkway to her front door is simply an extension of that paved parking spot. The whole space feels bigger because she has not separated parking from garden. She has also not put up a fence between her and her neighbor. She has created, with them, a semitransparent screen so the space breathes and feels open and less confining than it would were there a hedge or fence between Porter and her neighbor.

Look closely and you'll also see that she used the same paving material for the driveway, the walkway to the front steps and the path leading down the side of her house. The space feels more expansive than it really is.

She then placed a lot of pots on the walls and steps up to the front door in order to bring detail, interest and vitality to her guests' arrival while at the same time separating the more Spartan look of the driveway surface from the decorated steps up to her front door.

FIGURE 2.3 *Suzanne Porter, a garden designer in Berkeley, California, created her own entry garden through a skillful use of striking plants that take attention away from the nearby parking slot. She separated sidewalk from garden with thorny barberry but then immediately planted the ornamental Autumn Moor Grass (Sesleria autumnalis) on both sides of the path to the front door to soften the effect. This garden, as with all entry gardens, sets up a style that informs the design of side and back gardens.*

FIGURE 2.4 *Cyndy and Gerry Prozzo, who live in southern Vermont, asked me to help them create an entry garden that would do two things: separate cars from the view by their front door and visually link their entry garden to the nearby Vermont woods.*

Because Porter's car is often in this parking spot, she provides a personal path that runs on the diagonal through her entry garden between sidewalk and front door. This path of irregular fieldstones and pea stone (see figure 1.4) leads guests right into the midst of the unusual plants that make up her entry garden, plants that draw attention away from the parked car. And because her neighbor, Anne Leyhe, who worked with *Horticulture Magazine* for years, is also a gardener, they fuse their gardens into one along their shared boundary line, thereby making each garden feel bigger.

Use the Power of the Path to Help You Design

When I designed an entry garden for Cyndy and Gerry Prozzo in southern Vermont years ago (figure 2.4), there were only a few shrubs in front of the brown-painted house and a lawn on the raised area in front of Gerry's studio (to the right). What we all wanted to create, given that the house was settled into a woodland edge, was a woodsy garden. My first decision was where to locate the path from the beige pea-stone parking area to the front door. By taking down part of the previously rectilinear stone wall and turning it into a lower, curving wall, I could sweep guests right around what had been a right angle.

Once around that sweep, I used large stepping-stones in a fairly straight line to draw people to the front door within the portico you can see in the background of the photo. Choosing large stepping-stones for the path material, each surrounded by ground-hugging Irish moss (*Sagina subulata*), helped me underpin the naturalistic feeling the Prozzos wanted throughout their entry garden.

Where path and stone wall curved, I placed a white birch under-planted with a mix of evergreens and flowering perennials. I placed a second birch up on the level by Gerry's studio and a third over by the front door. I then planted low perennials along both sides of the walk-way and slightly taller shrubs as we got further away from it. The path itself, as well as the Big Idea of a woodsy garden, helped me make decisions regarding plant choice and layout.

A Garden between House and Driveway

Look closely at figure 2.5 and take a moment to compare this and figure 2.4, the photo of the Prozzo entry garden, to find out if you can, in fact, see how similar these two gardens are. (You are thinking like a garden designer if you do.) The house and garden in figure 2.5, outside Portland, Oregon, are also in a woodland setting. Like the Prozzos, the owners/designers used pea stone and finely crushed stone as the surface for their driveway. But, as you will see in all the photos in this chapter, the owners did not want cars and the driveway to domi-nate the front of their house the way it so often does in American front

FIGURE 2.5 *Take up some of your excess driveway near your house and put a garden into the space, as the owners did here outside their home in Portland, Oregon.*

yards. First, they designed a carport that you can see on the far-left side of their home so they had a place to park their car well out of sight of the entry garden to the right. Second, to separate guests' parked cars from view when in the entry area at the right end of the house, they created a long island bed between the broad driveway/parking area and house. They then planted a striking garden of azaleas and a single upright tree along the back of their entry garden and an extraordinary thyme bed in front of those woody plants. By curving a stepping-stone path, they sweep guests through a front garden while preventing them from seeing deep into the entry courtyard until they arrive at the gateway into it.

So what do you do with this information, this description of a garden that is in all likelihood very different from yours? Here are a few principles:

> *Take up some of the driveway between your house and driveway to make an entry garden where paving used to be.*

> *Separate the driveway from the area around the front door with shrubs, perennials, perhaps even a tree to set your house into a garden that feels separate and a world apart from your driveway.*

> *Don't use the same material on your driveway that is used for the walkways to the doors of your house; cars do not equal people.*

> *Design the path from driveway to front door so it curves and therefore does not frame a view of parked cars.*

A New Use for an Unused Garage

Most Americans do not use garages for cars. They have become recycling centers; storage units for hoses, lawn mowers and garden equipment; places to keep the rubbish. As you can see in figure 2.6, designers Buell Steelman and Rebecca Sams, based in Eugene, Oregon, have accepted that fact and co-opted their garage into their garden. What they have done is something you also need to find a way to do: prevent cars, driveway and parking area from overwhelming the spirit and feeling of your front garden.

FIGURE 2.6 *By turning their garage into a design studio, designers Steelman and Sams anchored a welcoming entry garden that runs right out to their sidewalk in Eugene, Oregon.*

First of all, they blocked entry into what was a garage with a low stone wall so they now park on the street or in that small one-car slot. The garage is now a useful design studio and the anchor for the entry garden. By extending the stone retaining wall on both sides of the parking area to support gardens on either side, they have surrounded this one parking slot and the entire front of house and garage with a profusely blooming garden.

Secondly, they placed a set of steps into the right-most wall to draw people from the parking area up onto a new garden level as well as onto the path to their front porch under the deep overhang of the roof you see in the picture. This path in turn leads down a long side garden. Even in this densely populated area, family and guests can explore this private garden separated from street and neighbors across the street because of the height of plants in the front garden.

But notice, as in the Marchants' garden in figure 2.1, that the entrance garden outside of the frame to the left also leaps right over this parking slot and picks up again on the right side of the parking area, thereby setting this house, ex-garage and parking slot into a long, narrow garden.

Built Planters Separate Driveway from Entry Garden

Another problem with any driveway is that it often intrudes into the privacy of an entry garden. UPS and FedEx drivers can pull into your driveway just as readily as you can. Your job as an entry-garden designer is to separate the semipublic driveway from the private garden gathered around your front door. Figure 2.7 suggests how wooden planters can help, especially if your front door is close to your driveway. To fully understand this image, know that photographer Saxon Holt was standing at the beginning of the walkway to the front door of this home in San Anselmo in northern California when he looked back at the driveway to take this photo.

Sometimes built structures such as planters or fencing can solve problems plants can't handle. By installing trim-looking planter boxes on both sides of the parking slot, the owners were able to create two spaces: a garden outside a wing of the house to the left and a more private entry garden afforded by trees and underplantings in the planter boxes to the right. To visually link house to garden, the owners constructed the planter boxes of wood that echo the materials of this Shingle-style home.

One other point you can take away from this image is to give only a minimum amount of space over to driveway and turnaround areas. Remarkably enough, the average American two-car garage and driveway takes up around 2,200 square feet of property. That square-foot

FIGURE 2.7 *The restrained use of materials near house and garage creates focus rather than an incoherent mix of too many materials. Gray cedar siding on house and planters pleasingly contrasts with the brick driveway to unify this entry garden.*

figure is roughly equal to the square footage of living space in most American homes. These cars have to be put in their proper place, out of sight of our entry gardens.

Figure 2.8 offers an alternative to planter boxes: a fence. Perhaps your driveway leads to a garage set somewhat away from the house, as you see in this picture. Installing a fence appropriate for the style of your house—here, a white picket fence is perfect when installed near a gray house with white trim—helps separate driveway from front door and gardens. By running the fence parallel with your driveway yet set back from its edge two to three feet, you can plant between driveway and fence, as well as along the back of the fence, to create a rich, delicate separation between driveway and entry garden. The picket fence also provides a setting for an arbor through which you and your guests can walk from driveway to path to front door. How impersonal this would all look if you were to remove fence, arbor, roses and perennials and just have lawn running up to driveway edge. All of these elements—planting beds along both sides of white fence, arbor, roses, flowering perennials—increase the feeling of entry, arrival and welcome as your guests leave their parked cars and walk into an entry garden.

FIGURE 2.9 *In cooperation with plantswoman Michelle Chambers, landscape architect Dickson DeMarche from Wilton, Connecticut, created this entry garden for clients on the shore in Westport, Connecticut. The gray house gives rise to gray stone walkways; vertical trees answer the vertical house; mounding deciduous and evergreen shrubs contrast with all the vertical and horizontal lines, none of which draws undue attention from the remarkable view.*

Parking near the Front Door

Sometimes it is simply not possible or desirable to park cars well away from the front door. If that's the case with you, the layout of driveway, guest parking and entry garden/walkway in figure 2.9 has some ideas for you. This entry garden outside a home in Westport, Connecticut, relies almost totally on low-maintenance trees and evergreen shrubs. Landscape architect Dickson DeMarche provides a surface of granite cobble edged with the same material for guests who want to park close to his front door. As they get out of their car, they step up onto a bluestone-paved walkway that runs along the front of the parking area and through an elegant, restrained garden of evergreen and deciduous shrubs and birch trees.

The shorn mugho pines and the birch tree growing between the front door and the parking area screen cars from view. The trees act as tall, vertical elements in the entry garden and set the house into the landscape while the branches of the birch arch over the walkway to form a living roof over that part of the entry garden. Without those trees, this tall house would loom over guests.

Another thing to notice is how restrained, how elegant the plantings are. DeMarche has chosen five or six trees as vertical elements rising out of mounded evergreens, a cutleaf maple, a mass of *Hydrangea* 'Annabelle' punctuated by deftly placed ornamental grasses, and sedums. The bluestone path draws you toward the house; lush green lawn paths draw you into the garden. The restraint of this entry garden with its interplay of horizontals, verticals and mounds acts as a quiet foreground to the remarkable horizontal views in the background.

DESIGN PRINCIPLES

ᴄᴡ *The driveway and parking area can often help you find a good location for the beginning of your path; the front door of your house is, of course, its destination.*

ᴄᴡ *The driveway may well provide you with at least one edge for your new entry garden. Edges are important in these early stages of garden design.*

ᴄᴡ *Do what you can to screen the view of the driveway from the front door and from within your new front garden; a view of cars is not what a welcoming garden is all about.*

ᴄᴡ *Reduce the amount of driveway to the bare minimum.*

ᴄᴡ *Plant on both sides of your driveway, or at least one side of it, so that the visual interest upon arrival home is not on the driveway itself, but on your garden.*

ᴄᴡ *If you have a long driveway that leads directly to the face of a garage, curve the driveway so as you drive along it, you get glimpses of the house. A long, straight driveway directly to the garage door makes arrival at your home utilitarian and hard.*

ᴄᴡ *Simple yet elegant entry gardens between parking area and front door can be conceived as a set of vertical trees, mounding evergreens and massed perennials, through which a broad path can run between parking and front door.*

Chapter 3
Walkways to the Front Door

CHAPTERS 1 AND 2 introduced you to broad concepts: the style of your entry garden and its edges, particularly as they gather around driveway/parking. This more practical chapter is about the actual path between driveway and front door.

Paths are useful design tools. They break big areas down into smaller, more easily designed spaces. They link previously separate places, and in doing so act as the spine of a garden with plants going up in height the further they get from either side of the path. Curves or junctions in paths suggest places for trees or shrubs so that your paths curve or split just there for a reason. The placement of trees provides places for shrubs under them. The beginning and end of paths provide places for ornaments, planted pots and other welcoming details. The path is the place where all good garden design starts.

Go out your front door and look out toward the driveway to where you park your car. Do you already have a path linking driveway to front door? Is it serviceable, appropriately located, welcoming? If you don't have a front path, look from the vantage point of your front door to see where guests invariably walk to get to it.

Now walk out to the driveway/parking area and look back at the front of your house, especially the front door. Your job, in this, your first design gesture, is to determine where the path will run so that guests unfamiliar with your house know exactly where you want them to go. The style as well as direction, location, width, length and materials of this path are all central to the success of your entry garden.

Before reading on, thumb through the images in this chapter or in this whole book to get a sense of this path from driveway to front door so you can see the many options that are open to you. Notice all

(FACING) FIGURE 3.1 *When the path between parking area and front door runs parallel with the nearby wall of the house, you create rectilinear gardens, the shapes of which marry house to garden. Design by Dan Borroff, Seattle, Washington.*

the shapes, colors and materials paths can be made of and the feeling each creates. Keep your own house and driveway in mind because one picture might well be the key to your path to the front door. And, again, remember that I have organized the pictures in each chapter from most formal to least formal. Where will your garden lie along that range?

The key to path design is to establish useful, logical beginning and end points. The front door is clearly the destination for the path from the place where you park; the driveway is its destination when you leave the house. You have no choice regarding the placement of the front door; you have some choice regarding where your entry path meets driveway.

It's also helpful to know that a straight path reflects the straight lines of your house and therefore tends to marry the lines of the house to those of the garden. But if you are prepared to give up all lawn at the front of the house, as all the gardens show in this chapter, curving or broadly arcing paths feel right wandering through a richly planted garden. Generally a straight path has clarity, force and strength; a curving path has grace, flow and mystery.

It's also helpful to know about the hierarchy of materials from which paths can be made. Tightly fitted rectangular or square-cut stones are, on the scale from formal to casual, most formal. They are most appropriate when you want to make a clean-edged straight path (see figure 3.1). Brick is the next step down on that hierarchy, followed by tightly fitted fieldstones, embedded concrete, stepping-stones or wood. Do not use lawn for your path to the front door as it gets wet, even muddy, and demands all sorts of maintenance. Do not use crushed gravel as it will track into your house on the soles of shoes. And finally, do not use wooden rounds; when wet or coated in frost, they are slippery and unsafe.

Let's look at some alternatives for paths through front gardens that link sidewalk or driveway to front door. And please remember that it's *not* helpful to think about whether you like these gardens or not; it *is* helpful to think about what you can learn from them.

Cut Stones Lead to Straight Lines

Figure 3.1 shows a small entry garden Dan Borroff designed for his clients in Seattle, Washington. The first thing you may notice about this path (and the related retaining walls) is that it is comprised of right angles, all of which are parallel or perpendicular to those of the house. One result of these straight lines is that house and garden share those lines, and are therefore drawn into a visual relationship with one another. Test this design against the layout of the space between your parking area and front door. Would low retaining walls help you create a level rather than sloping path to your front door? Does the idea of a straight rather than curving path fit your style?

Another thing you can learn from this garden is that a house (and your entry garden) looks best when the garden or lawn in front of it is also level. A level garden and path feels like an extension of the first floor of your house; a garden and path that slopes away from the house feels separate. Furthermore, people like to walk on level surfaces. Here, the designer used this low retaining wall to create that level space on which people can comfortably walk. The retaining wall also establishes the logical edges of this garden, and increases the feeling of privacy gathered around the front door.

Next, notice that Borroff has designed an entry path with two right angles in it. As guests walk up the sloping panel of cut slate, they turn left into the first right angle and up steps, then walk a bit before turning right to approach a second set of steps up to the front door. One result of designing the path this way (rather than running it straight from door to sidewalk) is that when the owners open their front door, they look into a garden of trees underplanted with shrubs and perennials rather than down a straight path leading to the sidewalk.

Another important point is that the house, as well as all the stone used in path, steps and walls, are dark gray. The lesson to take away is not the color gray, but the fact that the color of your house helps you choose the color of the material for your entry path and any walls that might be associated with it. Plant choice and layout can then complement or contrast with the material of the path. Look at the other pictures in this chapter and you will see how compatible the materials are between house, path and plants in a well-designed front garden.

One final thing to learn from this image is that if the face of your house is tall, a tree or trees near the front door will help make the space around the front door cozier. Rather than have the face of the house loom overhead, plant a tree near it, and its branches will arch over the front-door landing.

FIGURE 3.2 *Plants indigenous to or associated with the stark Arizona landscape are just right for this minimalist garden. The pink-flowering* Verbena tenuisecta *in the foreground contrasts with the round pads of the opuntia cactus in the middle ground and the upright and thorny ocotillo* (Fouquieria splendens) *in the background.*

Big Steps, Big Landings

Even though this house and minimalist garden in figure 3.2 are in Tucson, Arizona, there are many lessons to be learned as you develop the design for the path through your entry garden. Whether your house is in Arizona or not, consider using large, rectangular stones or panels of tinted concrete to lead from your parking area to the front door in a dramatic way. Here, tinted concrete that matches the color and starkly beautiful style of the house has been used, but you could use big slabs of cut Pennsylvania bluestone or western sandstone, depending on where you live in North America. Big, flat stones and steps up to a broad, long landing to the front door might be just the thing for your house.

Even though figures 3.1 and 3.2 show you two options regarding the use of straight paths in your entry garden, there is a big difference in the feeling created by the straight lines in these two gardens. By staggering the edges of the white steps in figure 3.2, the designer creates opportunities to integrate plantings and path. As the pink-flowering verbena in the foreground grows, it will gradually fill that right angle and flop onto the step, thereby integrating step and plant. You could do the same by offsetting steps one from the next so you can plant in those offsets, as you see here. Further integration results between steps, path and garden when the designer does not level the natural, gentle slope of the land with a retaining wall but sets the steps into it.

One last point to keep in mind is that color has a lot to do with emotion. When you choose materials for your path, keep in mind that dark gray and white, as you see in these first two photographs, are visually cool colors and so they visually cool down a garden. Furthermore, a dark gray stone path in full sun literally absorbs and holds heat while the white material for house and path in Arizona reflects sunlight, thereby keeping surfaces cooler.

A Curving Brick Path

Cut stone or large concrete slabs set in straight lines have a degree of formality and strength that might be just right for your home and style. Brick, being a smaller material with a terra-cotta color, is a warmer, more comforting material for a path. Because individual bricks are small, they are versatile; you can lay them in a variety of ways to create straight or curving paths. In the garden of Charles and Kathryn Brumder, who live in Hartland, Wisconsin (figure 3.3), you see a gently curving brick path that draws guests clearly and comfortably from the parking area to the front door. The simple flow of this path works quietly and freely in this small garden to show guests the way. It does not have the drama of the concrete path in figure 3.2, nor should it. This home in Wisconsin does not have the architectural flourishes, nor is it set in such a dramatic landscape as that of Arizona. That is not to say one path is better than the other; each is right for the indigenous landscape and the architecture of the house. Not only is this brick path open; so is the garden through which it runs.

This brings us to a very important point about the nationwide interest in the entry garden. My feeling is that the new American garden is about walking among our plants, not walking past them. Too often in America we plant only one side of a path to the front door (or neither side), so we end up walking past plants. When you plant both sides of the path as the Brumders have done here, you walk *through* a garden and *among* your plants.

Another point to consider for your entry garden and the path through it is how to resolve existing slopes between front door and driveway: with ramps, sloping paths or with retaining walls, steps and level paths. You'll notice in figure 3.1 that the designer gently sloped the broad ramp leading from sidewalk to the first set of steps. He then built a retaining wall to support level steps and level path to the front door. The designer in figure 3.2 used no ramps, only level steps and path, yet allowed the land on either side of steps and path to slope away from the house.

In figure 3.3, you see that the area at the front of this house is virtually flat, yet the designer created a five-inch step up onto a perfectly

level walkway to steps to the front porch. A sloping path would have been possible, but that little step makes all the difference. When you step off of the gray concrete driveway and onto the brick path, you feel you have left the semipublic world of the driveway and are entering a private garden. These details are subliminal, yet compelling.

There is another important lesson to be learned in figure 3.3 that gathers around lighting. Look closely at this picture and you might get a model for lighting your entry path. First, you'll see a low light fixture just to the right of the first step. Next, you'll see one to the left of the lower porch step; then there are the ceiling fixtures running the length of the covered porch; finally there are two wall sconces on each side of the front door. All four of these light sources combine to create a safe, well-lit entry path and garden. Make sure your path is well lit too, but do not force people to look directly into floodlights or spotlights as they walk from driveway to front door. Keep the lighting subtle and indirect as the Brumders did here.

FIGURE 3.3 *The white-blooming* Hydrangea *'Annabelle' provides a backdrop for this June garden of pink astilbes and hardy geraniums as well as the chartreuse blooms of* Alchemilla mollis *in Hartland, Wisconsin.*

FIGURE 3.4 *Halian lavender (Lavandula stoechas) to the right, English lavender (L. angustifolia) in the path's curve, Coreopsis verticillata 'Zagreb', Clematis × jackmanii climbing up the lamppost, iris, rose, yucca and other flowering plants welcome guests to this home in Franklin, Tennessee.*

Pebble-Embedded Concrete Paths

Concrete, being a liquid, takes virtually any shape, and so becomes an appropriate material for a curving path from front driveway to front door. Because it is a liquid, you can also embed pebbles into the wet concrete in a wide range of colors, sizes and textures. As you can see in figure 3.4, designer Mike Hayes used embedded concrete to form the curving path to the front door of the Pearces' home in Franklin, Tennessee. Here is a fine example of how you can turn an unsympathetic material like concrete into a pleasing walkway between driveway and front door: by embedding beige pebbles into the surface of a newly poured walk. By curving such an embedded path around low, woody shrubs as you see here, you prevent guests from seeing the whole path from any one point, thereby diminishing the negative visual impact that too much concrete seen all at once might have on your entry garden.

The fact that Hayes planted the fragrant-leaved lavender in the curve of this path brings up a good point for your entry path; plant a fragrant-leaved or fragrant-flowering shrub in that curve so that anyone walking along that path will brush against it to release its pleasing scent.

Now, take a closer look at the house. There are several things about it that could have given rise to a formal garden: the tall window to the left; the columns on each side of the portico; the finely detailed and impressive front door. Yet look at the garden and you see approachable, informal, relaxed plantings of perennials and shrubs associated with an English cottage garden: roses, lavender, iris, coreopsis and clematis, among others. Clearly the owners wanted to tone down the formality of their home by using these plants on both sides of their curving, pebble-embedded concrete path. Having said that, they added a formal note of symmetry by planting that pair of Dwarf Alberta spruces on each side of the entry landing. These two evergreen plants act as a kind of liaison or coupler between the formal architecture and informal garden. All of these points can be springboards for your own thinking about how you can gather a garden on both sides of your path to the front door.

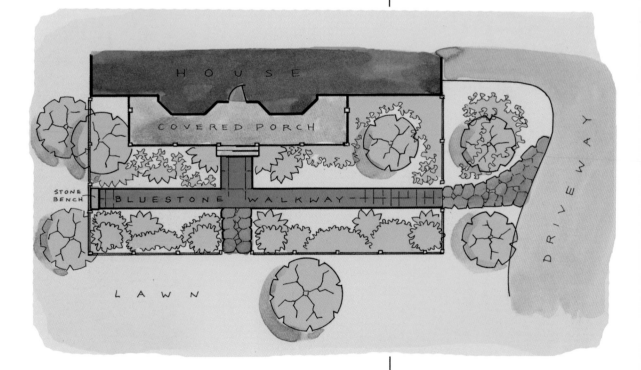

ORNAMENTS NEAR THE FRONT DOOR

❧ Ornaments in an entry garden underpin the mood and style of your garden while also hinting at the style inside your home.

❧ The best garden ornaments are those that relate to you and your family. When you choose ornaments that have personal associations—your grandmother's birdbath, your father's antique rake, or a reference to horses because you have one—then the ornament feels right and perfect for your garden.

❧ As with pots, you can place garden ornaments on one or both sides of entries and steps, near benches or chairs, at curves in paths or right by the front door. Look at figures 1.1, 3.3, 3.4, 3.6, 4.3, 4.8, 7.2, 10.6, and 10.7 and you'll get lots of ideas about how to site ornaments in your entry garden.

(ABOVE) FIGURE B *Look at figure 7.2 and you'll see the whole façade of this home in Vermont. You will then more fully understand how this charming gathering of ornaments feels absolutely right for this entry. This old unpainted clapboard house with the traditional unpainted picket fence enclosing the entrance garden bespeak the passage of time. The owner, Anne Marie Jensen, chose ornaments by her front door that relate to the feeling and style both outside and inside her home.*

(RIGHT) FIGURE C *This antique child's wagon underpins the feeling of warmth and charm you feel in this entry garden outside a house in Portland, Oregon. Old objects in new gardens impart a sense of time and age.*

FIGURE 3.5 *Sue and Ed Muszala created this garden in front of the home where they used to live in Bridgewater, Connecticut. Sue told me she started the garden by planting annual ageratum along both sides of the path; the rest was lawn. With each gardening year, the lawn got smaller, the garden bigger.*

The Stone Carpet

Look back at the four photos in this chapter and you will see there is a strict edge between solid, hard-edged paths and the plants that make up the garden. The path in figure 3.5 shows you a way to soften that edge, to integrate path and garden plants. The Muszalas, who live in northwestern Connecticut, chose to lay down an informal stone carpet from their driveway to front door. This path is made up of irregular fieldstones that are laid with gaps between the stones for ground-hugging plants such as thyme and lawn grass. The outer edge of such a path is also irregular so plants from the adjacent garden can creep in between stones, thereby integrating path and plants.

Even though the garden feels informal and ebullient, there are several structural elements along the path that you could incorporate into your entry path to make the abundance of your entry garden take on a bit of form. As in figure 3.4, a pair of shrub conifers are planted on each side of the portico. These firming, structural notes are repeated in the pair of potted upright evergreens under the roof of the portico. These four evergreens provide an unchanging, uniform, green background against which to take the measure of the ever-changing perennial garden.

FIGURE 3.6 *Jan Nickel's entry path is a curvilinear boardwalk that sweeps people through her densely planted entry garden to a broad, generous landing by the front door. Whether your path is of wood, stone or brick, it could curve like hers through a garden that runs from house to driveway.*

Another structural element has been brought into play along each edge of the path, illustrating the central role the path can play. The path acts as the spine of your entry garden, and as such can help you choose plants along it, a decision that has implications for what you plant well away from the path as well. Notice how the lower plants are near the path, and the further you get away from it, the taller the plants get. That alone is of great help when it comes to choosing plants for your entry garden. Now look closely at how plants are laid out along the path. The owners have planted the chartreuse-blooming Lady's Mantle (*Alchemilla mollis*) in the foreground and then at various points along both sides of the entire path. This repeated color and form along path edge lends coherence to the garden. Now notice how the white, as well as pink, blooming astilbes are also repeated near the beginning, middle and end of the path. What you see in this July garden is a theme gathered around white, pink and chartreuse. The result of all these design elements is that this garden holds together. It has coherence and a calm, unconstrained structure. That's good gardening.

There is no question that walking along this entry path and through this garden of perennials and woody plants would be a pleasure. But that pleasure lies not only in the plants and the relaxed path through them, but also in the destination of this path. The flat face of this two-story house is made more approachable by the addition of the portico over the front door. Porticoes offer enclosure of a human scale; a sheltering roof overhead; and a clear, welcoming destination for your entry path. If the front of your house feels imposing or lifeless, a portico appropriate for the style, color and materials of your house might make the area around your front door more welcoming.

The Wooden Walkway

Wood is also a sympathetic material for a path, one that is especially appropriate when leading to a wooden house in a rural, woodsy setting such as Jan Nickel has (figure 3.6). As you saw in figure 2.2, Nickel starts her path to the front door at the edge of her guest parking area with a set of wooden steps that turns into a curving and gently sloping boardwalk that runs through her extensive entry garden.

A wooden walkway, even when built close to the ground, has the effect of lifting you just a bit above the garden. Nickel used the curving boardwalk to help guests wend their way through her garden so they can take in the full experience of arriving at her home.

Notice in figure 3.6 how important the tree to the left of the picture is in breaking up that expansive mansard roof when the house is seen from the boardwalk. There is an important point here for you. As you walk from your driveway to the front door, pay attention to that vast expanse of roof (and wall) that exists on any house. As you walk the length of your proposed path, consider where trees might be placed to keep the roof from making the arrival at your front door visually heavy.

There is one final universal design principle Nickel has used that you need to pay attention to no matter what material your entry path is made of. She has held to a roughly four-foot width along the entire length of her path, but when she gets to the area around her front door, she broadens the wooden path into a generous landing. As your entry path approaches the all-important front door, expand whatever material your path is made of to create a broad, open space where several people can gather, where you can set out planted pots, garden ornaments and other details that will hint at the life lived inside your home, just as Jan Nickel did.

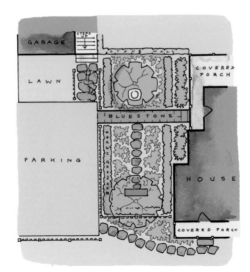

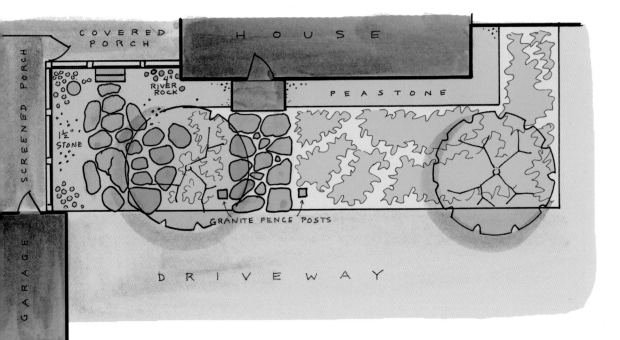

The diagram shows a landscape plan with labels: COVERED PORCH, HOUSE, SCREENED PORCH, GARAGE, 4" RIVER ROCK, 1½" STONE, PEASTONE, GRANITE FENCE POSTS, DRIVEWAY.

DESIGN PRINCIPLES

∽ *The path itself is where you begin to design your garden; get the path right and your garden will flow with it.*

∽ *Straight paths are forceful, assertive, firm elements in the landscape that often relate better to the geometry of a house than curving paths do.*

∽ *Curving paths need to curve in broad, simple ways. Curving paths often enable you to screen unsightly views and they also help you build mystery along the way.*

∽ *Paving materials exist on a scale from formal to informal: cut stone and brick to embedded concrete to stone carpets and wood. Knowing this range helps you choose the right path material for your entry garden.*

∽ *Entry paths need to be safe and well lit.*

∽ *Houses like to sit on a level plane. Paths and related stone retaining walls can help establish this level plane, one that reads like an extension of the first floor of your house.*

∽ *Curves in entry paths are good places for fragrant plants. As people walk the curve, they brush against the fragrant leaves or flowers to release the aroma.*

∽ *Paths can help you choose plants: low plants along the edges, with plants getting taller as you move away from the path. The entrance to a path is an appropriate place for a tree or shrubs to mark the entrance.*

Chapter 4
Gardens around the Front Door

THE BEST PLACE to start your entry garden is right around the front door. By starting there rather than planting broad beds along the length of your entry path or at the driveway end of your path, you will feel more comfortable as you tackle this more manageable space. Once you get the garden around the door established, you can build out from there in a series of comfortable stages, each of which can be made to feel complete. Let's take a close look at six small gardens right by the front door.

A Small Garden in Front of a Big House

The owners of this classic home built in 1925 in Oregon, created an equally classic garden along the path to, and then right around, their front door (figure 4.1). By leaving most of their easily maintained front lawn intact, they were able to keep their entry garden of a manageable size. To see the front garden in the context of the whole front yard, turn ahead to figure 5.1.

In one simple, elegant gesture, the owners planted a low boxwood hedge set back just two feet from each side of the path from their driveway all the way to, and then across, the front of their house. This low, easily maintained hedge forms the backdrop for a gathering of low perennials and annuals along the length of the path. Notice how the owners planted the same low boxwood hedge as a background for the garden around their front door and then repeated the same boxwood trimmed to a sphere nearby. Having established this structure, the owners planted low, broad-leaved shrubs, hardy geranium, sweet william, and annual nicotiana for color and detail. They then installed window boxes and, to create a visual link between the low boxwood hedges and

(FACING) FIGURE 4.1 *A dignified house gives rise to a dignified garden around the front door of this house in Oregon. Boxwood and begonias, hardy geraniums and verbenas, nicotianas and pansies, all combine with evergreens in the ground and in pots to form an elegant welcome for guests.*

the window boxes, they repeated small boxwoods at either end of each window box before filling the balance of the boxes with begonias.

The year-round structure provided by the boxwood hedge and spheres is reinforced by other symmetrically placed evergreen shrubs both in the ground and in pots. Look closely and you'll see a matched pair of cast-stone pots planted with small evergreens on both sides of the front door, as well as a matched pair of chartreuse-leaved arborvitae planted directly into the front garden on each side of the front door.

This firmly structured yet lively planting of evergreen shrubs, annuals and perennials results in a small garden that feels appropriately restrained for the nature of this dignified home.

A Small Garden around Big Front Steps

While the first floor of some homes is only a step or two above the grade of the front garden, perhaps the front door of your home is set higher and can only be reached by a set of two, three, four or more steps. As you can see in figure 4.2, you can use those steps not only to display planted pots, but also as an anchor for a small garden on both sides of the steps and the path leading to them.

The key to a garden on both sides of a set of steps is to make them feel accessible and welcoming, not remote and challenging. The Brinks, who live in Vancouver, British Columbia, have created a welcoming garden that tames this formidable set of steps in a number of ways, all of which might be of interest no matter how many steps you have leading up to your front door.

First, there are several architectural elements that lighten the look of what could appear as an imposing entry into the Brinks' home. The steps themselves are not made of stone, brick or other heavy materials; they are made of wood. The cheek walls that frame the steps are clad in the same clapboard as those on the walls of the house, so there is a visual and physical connection between house and steps. While most of the risers and treads that make up the steps are painted dark gray, part of the riser of the top-most step is painted pink, in a lighthearted flight of fancy that visually lightens that top step. To further lighten the look, the front door is not solid but has an elegant ellipse-shaped

(FACING) FIGURE 4.2 *This private entry garden in British Columbia is inspired by the English cottage garden made up of campanulas, foxgloves, artemisias, poppies, lilies, feverfew, and even potted pansies and pelargoniums.*

window in it that breaks the mass of the door, thereby making it feel more approachable. I point out all these architectural details because oftentimes gardeners ask plants to do all this work. Plants can certainly help, but architectural changes are sometimes the first ones that need to be made to create a welcoming garden by the front door.

Now let's look at what the owners planted around these imposing steps. First, they installed a tree not all that far to the right, the branches of which arch over the steps to give the space above a scale of human proportion. Had the sky been the roof over this set of steps, they would have felt much more imposing, in part because the house would have loomed over guests as they started up the steps. The vine that grows to the left of the steps is another important element. It both visually and physically links the steps to the ground. The vine also covers a good deal of the house, thereby reducing the amount of front wall that visitors see as they walk up the steps. Visitors feel they are in a garden even as they climb these steps.

In many ways, the owners set the steps into a cottage garden. By planting familiar garden plants such as feverfew and poppy, campanula and foxglove, lily and sweet William, they created a simple, easy and welcoming feeling around each side of the steps. The color and detail in this cottage garden draws attention away from the steps, while the steps in turn provide various heights from which visitors can look down onto the garden. Furthermore, this garden hides a very high foundation and in doing so makes the house feel it is floating just above the garden. The entire look is lightened by perennials laid out in a familiar, informal way.

To further break up the mass of steps and wall near the front door, the owners placed planted terra-cotta pots both on the cheek walls as well as the steps. To add just a hint of contrasting formality and struc-ture, and to create just a hint of a garden on the top landing, they set a matched pair of evergreen topiaries on each side of the front door and then underplanted them with colorful annuals. The details embodied in tree and vine, annuals and perennials, architectural details and color, all combine to create a garden around this elevated front door.

Letting House Colors Suggest Garden Colors

If you are going to develop a small garden just around your front door, the color of that door as well as that of the path material become especially important. In figure 4.3 you see the design for a small entry garden that landscape architect Suzanne Arca created for her own house in the San Francisco Bay Area. Here, the rust-colored path from the driveway edge to the entry porch echoes the color of her front door. Arca even had the grouting between the walkway's fieldstones tinted so that the concrete complements the stones that it holds in place. The house, of course, is gray.

FIGURE 4.3 *Designer Suzanne Arca gathers grays and browns around a gray house with a brown door. She then adds unexpected touches of chartreuse to brighten the look.*

Now look at the colors of flower and foliage in the garden and you will see variations on those same browns and grays. Arca planted dark brown sedums and other succulents that retain soil in the crevices of the brownish rocks near the first step in the pathway. Colors in that same family of rusts, bronzes and browns reappear in a grass to the left and in the deep burgundy phormiums to both the right and left of the path. Bowls and urns set on the steps up to the entry porch are glazed almost the same color as the strap-like leaves of the phormium. The flowers of the perennials to the right and left of the path also throw a color within that same range.

Then there is the color gray, the dominant color of the house, which is repeated in the foliage of certain shrubs, perennials and ground covers throughout this small garden. To brighten what could have become a somber gray-and-rust-colored garden, Arca introduced startling chartreuse in both foliage and flower.

Coherence is a crucial element of small garden design, and by studying this photo you see several ways to establish coherence in your small space around the front door:

> *Choose plants that have flower and foliage colors within a limited range that will reflect or complement the colors of your house and pathway.*

> *Repeat those colors on both sides of the pathway in plants as well as in pots and ornaments.*

> *Choose a contrasting color to enliven the space if the color range feels too limited and boring.*

> *Tie the wall of the house to the garden with a vine.*

FIGURE **D** *This combination, gathered around different shades of purple in petunias, lobelia, and verbena, is knitted together by the gray leaves of* Helichrysum petiolare. *The gray leaves echo house color.*

WINDOW BOXES

Window boxes add charm, color and detail to the front of traditional houses, and can also break up the broad and possibly imposing façade of a house, but they do require a good deal of watering and fertilizing to keep them looking good. Because you don't want to block views from front windows, choose just a few upright plants that will grow no more than ten inches high; place trailing plants in front of them. Your house will help you decide what materials and colors to use in the construction of window boxes. Refer to figures 5.1 and 10.6 for more ideas.

An Entry Garden that Wraps Its Arms around You

If your front door snuggles into the ell of your house, where two wings of your house meet at a right angle, your house already forms two of the four sides of your small entry garden. That's a luxury few enjoy. As you see in figures 4.4 and 4.5, designer Shari Bashin-Sullivan took full advantage of the ell in this home in Oakland, California, when she designed this small entry garden.

By installing the low, curving stucco wall and gardens on both sides of it, she enclosed the space right around the front door. By tinting the stucco on this wall a color that echoes that of the house, she used the wall to visually link house to garden. So as not to draw undue attention to the pathway, she chose a muted, soft gray slate and then slightly tinted the grouting concrete so it wouldn't create a busy look on the ground. This vertical and horizontal hardscaping (as well as the corner of the house) provided Bashin-Sullivan with an appropriate structure in which to place lively plantings.

Now that you're beginning to understand more about how to discern garden design ideas from photos, take a break from reading my text to take a close look at figures 4.4 and 4.5 to see if you can pick up some of the design elements yourself. Ask "Why is that there?" of every element in these two photos even though you may not know the names of any of the plants. Once you've finished your own analysis, read my list of far-from-exhaustive observations:

> The glossy-leaved conical shrubs on each side of the entry add just a touch of formality and structure to the garden, and in doing so make the lack of formality in the rest of the planting appear intentional.
>
> The repetition of burgundy-red foliage throughout this design adds unity to the design while contrasting pleasingly with the orange undertones of the stucco house.
>
> The variegated grass on the right and the magenta impatiens both strike a remarkable chord of color to keep the design from feeling too pat.
>
> The soft orange terra-cotta pot echoes the color of the stucco walls of the house, thereby linking garden to house.

The feeling of welcome, the feeling of entry and arrival emanates from many sources: the gap in the stucco walls; the overhanging branch of the tree on the left; the vine overhanging the entrance to the porch; the widening of the path by the entry; the porch itself and the pots gathered within it; the colorful and enlivening variety of plants inside and outside that stucco wall that celebrates arrival; the well-tended garden that bespeaks pride and pleasure on the part of the owners.

Look at figure 4.4. Imagine that you are inside the house looking out through the blue-framed window on the right. Guests walk into this garden upon arrival; when in the house, they look out into it.

Add your list to mine and you've got a good primer on designing an entry garden in the ell of *your* house.

(FACING) FIGURE 4.4 *The entry is framed by a pair of shiny-leaved* Loropetalum chinense, *which contrast with the burgundy-leaved* Fuschia thymifolia *and the* Ajuga reptans 'Gaiety' *ground cover among other plants. Design by Shari Bashin-Sullivan of Enchanting Planting, Oakland, California.*

FIGURE 4.5 *The yellow-flowering abutilon to the right echoes the color of the stucco walls yet contrasts beautifully with the many dark green foliage plants. Both windows in this ell look out into a garden anchored by the large terra-cotta pot to the left. Notice how private this garden feels even though it is only twenty-five feet or so from the street.*

69 *Gardens around the Front Door*

A Long, Narrow Garden Running Parallel with the Front of the House

Rather than garden immediately around the door itself, consider the minimalist, low-maintenance design shown in figure 4.6 that runs across the front of the house. This garden, owned and designed by Richard Westmacott from Georgia, is based on a series of lines parallel with the front of the house. So that you can apply this design, get the front of your house in mind as I point to each of the lines in figure 4.6. The first line parallel with the front of the house itself is the five-foot-wide covered porch; second is the five-foot-wide planting bed at the base of the porch with the five brick steps coming down from the porch; third is a line of brick edging, then the swept path (a southern idiom) and then another line of brick edging. Next is the five-foot-wide planting of ground cover liriope, which is in turn held in place by the approximately five-foot-wide American Holly (*Ilex opaca*) hedge.

Contrasting verticality comes from the fragrant jasmine vines growing on the porch posts as well as the two large magnolia trees that shade and cool this entire entry garden.

No matter where you live, no matter what your house is like, no matter how big or long it is, you could apply this plan to make an entry garden that is manageable and attractive. The plant list is minimal: two types of ground covers, a vine, two trees and a path that runs to the front door as well as along the front of the house, and an evergreen hedge that is placed at least as far away from the house as the front wall of the house is tall.

That hedge has no end of implications. It creates a cooling sense of place between it and the front of the house; it screens views of nearby streets and sidewalks when you are sitting on the porch or looking out through your front downstairs windows; it acts as a backdrop for a flower garden at its front and back; it creates a high degree of privacy along the front of your house, offering a space where you could even design a sitting area out-of-view of passersby.

A Garden Running Straight to the Front Door

Jennifer Myers lives in an old German limestone farmhouse she restored at the back of a deep, narrow lot in Austin, Texas. Figure 4.7 shows just the part of the entry garden she designed around her front door. The first thing you notice, I'm certain, is the playful use of color: the periwinkle blue door and rocking chair, the orange terra-cotta pots, red annuals, green foliage, and the creamy white limestone on the ground and in the walls of the house to provide a quiet background for all this color.

Myers has created a beautifully balanced garden. Of course, there is quite a bit of symmetry in this garden—the layout of door and windows, the columns on both sides of the door, similar palms in similar pots, cast-stone pots on the second step up, the square pots in the foreground—but you don't come away with a feeling of rigidity. Even the path, with the front door, is the fulcrum point for all this symmetry and tones down the symmetry. Myers chose to lay an informal limestone-and-gravel path not only to echo the material of the house but also to offer an honest, warm welcome to her guests. (Had she laid tightly fitting square or rectangular pieces of limestone for her walkway, everything about this garden would have tightened up and felt rigid.) As you look at this picture, you feel pleasure in the color and vitality of her vision as well as the generous space she provides for that blue rocking chair and the black table across from it.

The style of maintenance also keeps this garden from showing the work. Myers is not bothered that bits of gravel have been scuffed onto the fieldstones. She's not bothered by the bit of green algae that has formed on the face of the steps or on some of her pots. If you maintain your garden too finely, it can feel stiff. Don't worry about getting and keeping everything perfect. You can maintain the life right out of your garden.

(FACING) FIGURE 4.7 *A truly broad landing by the front door gives you room for planted pots, a table, even a rocking chair. If the color of the walls and landing are muted, add all kinds of color. Design by owner Jennifer Myers, Austin, Texas.*

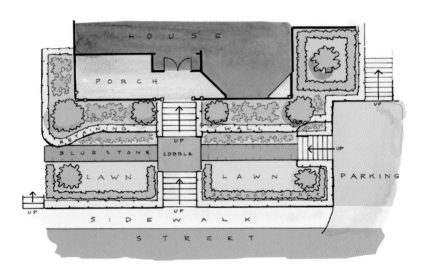

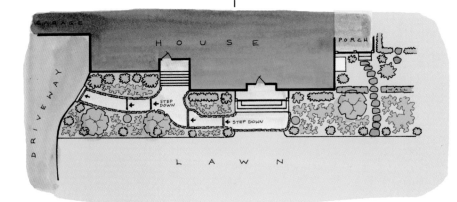

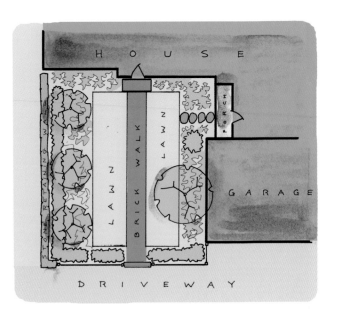

(FACING) FIGURE 4.8 *Magenta, red and pink seen against beige limestone, a periwinkle blue door and an abundance of dark green foliage—now there's a color combination for you. Design by owner Jennifer Myers, Austin, Texas.*

75 *Gardens around the Front Door*

Extending the Garden by Your Front Door

As I mentioned at the opening of this chapter, perhaps you want to start small by creating a garden just by the front door and then, over time, expanding your idea further out into the lawn, perhaps eventually out to sidewalk or street. To help you see how to do that, let's step back from Jennifer Myers' front-door garden to see how she expanded it toward the street. As you can see in figure 4.8, Myers has a lot more in mind than just what you see in figure 4.7, and when Karen Bussolini took this photograph she had only backed up to a point about a third of the way from the front door of Myers' house to the sidewalk. What Myers knew when she developed this long, narrow garden is that it reflected the long, narrow lot on which her house sat. By painting her door periwinkle blue, by gathering red flowers not only by the door but in the urn on the pedestal two-thirds of the way from sidewalk to front door, she attracted the attention of her guests down the length of her walkway.

Like the designs for many front gardens, paths run straight from sidewalk, street or driveway to the front door, and it is along that line that you can expand your front garden over the years. Myers understood this when she planted the columnar yaupon (*Ilex vomitoria* 'Will Fleming') every ten feet or so down the length of her entry walkway to form a corridor. To the right and left are rectangular panels of lawn that set off the geometric principles on which this entry garden is based.

So, the progression of thought she followed (and you could employ) to create this garden was the following steps:

1. *Run a path from sidewalk straight to the front door.*

2. *Provide a visual respite two-thirds of the way along the path that acts as a benchmark, a milestone on the way to the front door; mark that spot with a strong garden ornament.*

3. *Create drama along the walkway with vertical hollies that lie in dramatic contrast to horizontal lawn.*

4. *Set up an informal tone by choosing irregular limestone slabs and crushed gravel, or other indigenous materials, that echo the color of the limestone house, and thereby marry path and garden to house.*

5. *Choose Mexican terra-cotta urns and pots to contrast with the limestone color, material of the house and plants.*

6. *Add striking accents of flower color to tempt people to explore the full length of the entry path.*

7. *Use paint colors to set off the colors of flower and foliage.*

8. *Set out furniture so that guests feel they can sit in the entry garden.*

9. *Hedge off the entire front of the garden, out by the street, to make this an utterly private space.*

10. *Don't get too fussy with maintenance; let the garden be itself, but at the same time, keep its meaning intact.*

As you develop the garden just by your front door—whether it is like or completely different from Myers'—keep this progression in mind. It's a progression that builds from the Big Idea through to the path to plant choice (from big to medium to small) to detail.

DESIGN PRINCIPLES

∾ *Start with a small garden right around the front door and, over time, build out from it to create an entire front garden; start small, and build on your success.*

∾ *Be aware of the colors of your house, and use those same colors, and complements of them, in flowers, foliage and materials.*

∾ *Entry gardens need not be high maintenance: by massing low-maintenance plants, you can create a manageable garden.*

∾ *Lawn is easier to maintain than a perennial garden. Let the easily maintained front lawn buy you time until you can expand the garden right around the front door into something larger.*

∾ *You will see your small entry garden from inside the house as well as from outside. Use open-branched shrubs and small trees to help you screen the street from inside views yet allow views into your garden.*

∾ *Don't be afraid of color. Jennifer Myers sure isn't.*

Chapter 5
A Lot of Lawn, a Little Lawn

THE AMERICAN FRONT LAWN is as sacrosanct as Grandma's apple pie. For the past hundred years or so, we Americans have planted and tended front lawns that run from house to sidewalk because we think that's what we are supposed to do. Drive down any residential street in America—or look out your front window—and you'll see what I mean. The roots of the Front Lawn can, in large part, be traced back to Frederick Law Olmsted, the designer of Central Park in New York City, but also the designer of early suburban communities, especially outside Chicago. Olmsted set every home in his suburban communities a uniform thirty feet back from the street or sidewalk, planted foundation plantings to screen the high foundations of the Victorian homes of his day, and then designed lawn to sweep from the edge of that foundation planting down to the street or sidewalk.

He felt that these "democratic lawns," as he called them, would bring people together. Unlike the hedged, fenced, and therefore separate front gardens of England and much of Europe, Olmsted felt we Americans should share, be more open and allow neighbors and passersby to see our lovely homes, and wave to us as we sat on our front porches. Those were the days when forty people a day drove by in Model T Fords at sixteen miles an hour and waved. Today thousands of people drive by suburban homes every day at forty miles an hour, and they're all on cell phones. Life in suburban America has utterly changed over the last hundred years, yet we, and many municipal codes, have held to this outdated way of thinking about the Front Lawn. Whole industries have sprouted up around this sacrosanct space, not the least of which are those that market herbicides, pesticides and irrigation systems.

As bigger and bigger houses go up on smaller and smaller lots, it is time to rethink what role the front lawn actually plays in our lives. Rethinking the gardens at the front of your house is inextricably connected to what you will do with your lawn and how those decisions will play out with your neighbors. You will have to find your level of comfort as you develop that garden, planting trees, shrubs, and perennials between the sidewalk and the front of your house that will separate house from street. The decisions gathered around your new front garden may not be easy because of the emotional tie we and our neighbors have to this front lawn. But happily, there are many, many options between taking up all the lawn and taking up none of it.

FIGURE 5.1 *By creating a two-foot-wide planting bed on each side of the path to the front door, and then a ten-foot-wide bed along the entire front of the house, the owners of this home in Eugene, Oregon, have created an easily maintained entry garden that is in keeping with the dignity of the architecture.*

Leave A Lot of Lawn

Figure 5.1 shows you how to create an entry garden that enables you to leave the bulk of your front lawn in place. Plant a narrow garden across the front of the house—something most people do already—and then sweep that garden right down each side of the entry path—something few people do. By planting a narrow garden on each side of the walkway, you draw the spirit and the substance of the gardens along the front of your house right out to the sidewalk. Once you plant both sides of the path to the front door, you and your visitors walk through a garden to this front door and that's a whole lot more interesting than walking on a path through lawn.

Don't be too literal as you look at this or any photo in this book. Be creative. You might have a sloping lawn, large trees in the front yard and a curving path, yet many of the same principles of garden design shown in this picture can be applied to your very different garden. Plant each side of your entry path, but make the beds on each side of the path to your front door wider than are shown in figure 5.1. Rather than boxwood, use a low flowering shrub like *Daphne x burkwoodii* 'Carol Mackie'. Plant two small flowering trees on each side of the beginning of your path. Sweep your garden right along the sidewalk as well, as you'll see in the last three photos of this chapter. Think about figure 5.1. Manipulate it so that you see how the lessons to be learned in it can relate to your own house in your own neighborhood. You just might find a comfortable solution that enables you to create a lively entry garden while retaining a good deal of lawn.

Shape the Front Lawn on Each Side of the Path

Tim Callis, the designer of this garden in Provincetown on Cape Cod (figure 5.2) has taken a bigger bite out of the front lawn than the owners of the preceding garden. When Karen Bussolini, the photographer, took this photo, she was standing by an open gate set within a white picket fence that runs parallel with the nearby sidewalk to her right and left. Callis not only planted both sides of the walkway leading to the porch and front door, he also planted along the foundation of the front porch, down the outsides of the front lawn and then along the back of the picket fence. The result is that he surrounded two large panels of lawn with lush summer gardens. The two strong, shaped panels of lawn provide a foil, a contrasting uniform horizontal panel of green against which to admire all the flowers, foliage and textures that make up this richly colorful garden of long-blooming perennials.

The background for the design of this garden holds some valuable lessons for you. This is a makeover garden. When the owners of this home asked Callis for help, he worked with what was there: a narrow path, a tiny strip of garden on both sides of it and oddly shaped lawn on each side of the path. Callis widened the brick path considerably so visitors can walk down the length of the path while plants can spill onto its edges. By widening the beds and choosing long-blooming perennials and spring bulbs, he was able to bring more excitement into the walk to the front door. By shaping the two areas of lawn into simple shapes, he helped draw the whole garden together.

FIGURE 5.2 *This exuberant garden at the front of a home in Provincetown in Cape Cod, Massachusetts, sweeps around all four sides of the two lawn panels on each side of the entry path. Catmint, lilies, hydrangeas, foxgloves, California poppies, coreopsis and Bachelor's Buttons, among many other flowering perennials, provide a long season of bloom.*

FIGURE 5.3 *To determine the minimum depth of a bed along the front of your house, measure the height of the front porch or wall of your house and then flop that dimension down onto the ground. That dimension will ensure that garden and house are in proportion with one another. Design by Elizabeth Lear.*

Split the Lawn into Sections with Hedges

Figure 5.3 shows a garden in Easthampton, New York, designed by Elizabeth Lear. What you see here is an alternative to the omnipresent foundation planting comprised of evergreen shrubs along the front of the house. This is a garden, a mix of flowering perennials and annuals that provide a wide range of engaging colors, fragrances and textures in a bed that is nearly as wide as the front porch is tall. This idea alone is worth considering.

But there is a second idea in this picture that is even more powerful and has a lot to do with your front lawn. Can you see that hedge in the far-right corner of the picture? The placement of that hedge as it runs from the far corner of the porch out toward the street or driveway is radical for our conservative front lawn ethic. That hedge divides the front lawn into two parts just as the trellis at the far corner breaks the porch into two parts. Once you place such a hedge off one corner of your house and run it out to the sidewalk, you can plant perennial borders on each side of that hedge while dividing your front lawn into two areas for different uses.

Then you can get really radical and consider running another hedge from the other front corner of your house out to the sidewalk, thereby separating front lawn from driveway. The remaining lawn would be a big square or rectangle contained by hedges and perennial gardens. This could be the start of something big.

Terrace a Sloping Front Garden

Before I go one step further with a few words on figure 5.4—a garden designed by Ann Smith in Seattle—let me say one thing. I imagine you looking at this picture and saying to yourself, "That brick retaining wall and the steps down through it would only cost me $15,000. I'm off to the next picture." Don't get discouraged by the scale of this garden. Think about it. If you have a sloping front lawn, how could you realistically interrupt that slope with a twelve- to twenty-four-inch-high retaining wall of some material appropriate to your front garden? With that wall in place, you could then garden between the wall and the front of your house and leave the balance of the front lawn in place. You could then draw guests from your driveway along a curving path, as shown here, and up the steps to your front door.

The key to the success of this idea is to set that retaining wall in such a way that the resulting garden between house and wall is in

FIGURE 5.4 *By interrupting sloping lawn with a low retaining wall placed well out into that lawn, you can create a gently sloping entry garden, the angle of which helps you display flowering perennials. This garden in Seattle was designed by Ann Smith.*

proportion with the front of your house. That is, if the façade of your two-story house is eighteen feet high, set that retaining wall at least eighteen feet away from the foundation and parallel with it; good proportions result.

Plant along Foundation and Sidewalk; Leave the Lawn Between

Figure 5.5 shows a second garden design in Oakland, California, by Shari Bashin-Sullivan (see figure 4.5 for the other one). It holds several manageable ideas for you:

> Plant shrubs and perennials along the foundation of your house so that you create a straight-edged garden, the line of which runs parallel with the front of your house. The deeper you make the bed, the more of a garden it will become.

> Plant a straight-edged garden out by the street or sidewalk with shrubs, perennials, and maybe even trees. The edge of this bed that faces the house should be parallel with the front of your house, not the sidewalk or street.

> If your front yard slopes, consider leveling all or part of it with a retaining wall.

> If the edges of beds near the house and sidewalk are both parallel with the house, the resulting lawn between the two beds will be a strong rectangular shape, as you can see in figure 5.5.

> Break the geometric lawn shape with a sweeping curved path from sidewalk to steps up to your front door of whatever material is right for your house and garden.

> Underpin the visual link between garden-by-street and garden-by-house by placing similarly planted pots on both sides of the two entrances.

No matter how big your front lawn is, this idea creates a coherent garden because the rectangular shape of the central lawn draws two separate gardens into a relationship with one another. If, however, one bed is curvy and the other is straight, or both curve in unrelated ways, the relationship between the two beds breaks. Shape that lawn, no matter how much of it you decide to leave.

(FACING) FIGURE 5.5 By designing parallel planting beds along house and sidewalk, designer Shari Bashin-Sullivan created a rectangular panel of lawn between the two, thereby creating a coherent garden for her client in Oakland, California.

Add a New Garden Only along the Sidewalk

Figure 5.6 offers a variation on the theme suggested by figure 5.5. Perhaps you are loathe to let go of the foundation planting you've had in place for years, but you do want to separate your front lawn from the sidewalk or street. As you can see in this picture, if you install a fence or hedge that is right for your house, just as designer Carrie Thomas did for her clients in Oregon, you increase the privacy of your entry garden and you keep a good deal of your lawn. Look closely at what Thomas did.

> She chose a white picket fence because it felt appropriate in front of this unassuming suburban home.

> She positioned the fence a few feet back from the sidewalk edge but parallel with the front of the house so she could plant a garden, one that changes seasonally, for passersby.

> By running the fence parallel with the front and sides of the house, she created a rectangular lawn between existing foundation planting and fence.

> She chose a picket fence that has that graceful down/up sweep to the tops of the pickets to reduce the feeling of barrier between sidewalk and house.

> She painted the fence white to help tie house to garden by repeating the white trim color on the house.

> She repeated the tulips in the garden in pots as well to visually relate the outer garden to the inner one.

The result of these simple gestures means that Thomas held on to a good deal of lawn, but framed that lawn with personal gardens that make all the difference to the feeling of coziness and tranquility in this home's setting. Look back at figure 5.5 and you'll see how much these two gardens have in common.

(FACING) FIGURE 5.6 *Designer Carrie Thomas left a generous rectangular panel of lawn between foundation planting and fence for her clients in Eugene, Oregon. Such a fence and garden might be a good first step for you as you develop your entry garden.*

Lawn as Path

So far in this chapter I have looked at examples of straight-edged lawns that run parallel with the front of the house. Figure 5.7 shows a garden in Louisville, Kentucky, designed by Sharon Sandlin, that runs on the diagonal. Look closely and you will see that the lawn path runs on a bias from the entrance to the garden on the right to a path leading down the side of the house to the left. This lawn, which reads as a path because it's of uniform width, is purposeful and creates a link between entry garden and another garden path.

If this model appeals to you because you have a very small front lawn, you could proceed in a number of ways over the years. First, plant a rectangular bed out by the sidewalk so the remaining lawn between front bed and house takes on a meaningful shape. The next year, take up a bit more lawn so that the front bed is on a diagonal with the house. The third year, take up the lawn where the innermost bed is in the photo so that you complete the diagonal. In the process of making two beds on the diagonal, you create, by default, the panel of lawn that will act as a path between your two perennial gardens. Of course, the next step is to take out the remaining lawn and put in stepping-stones so you can have even more garden. Figure 3.5 shows you just what I mean.

FIGURE 5.7 *Sharon Sandlin is both the designer and gardener of this effusive entry garden in Louisville, Kentucky. When sitting on one of those rocking chairs, she cannot see any lawn, just a mass of lavender and daisies, coreopsis and daylilies, helenium and bee balm.*

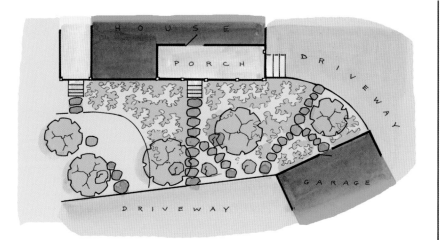

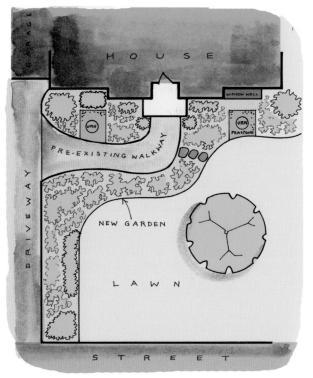

FIGURE 5.8 *By berming up their garden along the sidewalk in Austin, Texas, the Trimbles captured a bit more privacy and gave themselves even more surface on which to plant beds with* Lantana montevidensis, *two forms of Muhly Grass* (Muhlenbergia capillaris *and* M. lindheimeri), Salvia leucantha, *among many other flowering perennials and shrubs.*

Create a Bermed Bed

The Trimble garden in Austin, Texas (figure 5.8), is a variation on the theme set up by figure 5.7. Either may be a good model if you want to hold on to a bit of lawn but garden ambitiously on each side of it. The Trimbles' bit of lawn, made of buffalo grass (*Buchloe dactyloides*), which only needs mowing every three weeks or so, draws guests between the two luxuriant gardens made up primarily of drought-tolerant Texas natives.

The cultural theme that drove plant choice here was planting for drought-tolerance—xeriscaping. The visual theme for the plantings is the English cottage garden, and that, in turn, is set in motion to some degree by the pink-flowering Coral Vine (*Antigonon leptopus*) against the white house. That all-important vine not only complements the color of the house, but also sets up a color theme that drives color combinations: pink and white blooms interspersed with the gray foliage of low-mounding shrubs, gray ornamental grasses and the gray tones of the central buffalo grass lawn.

This topsoil berm in the foreground of figure 5.8 prevents precious rainwater from draining out of this garden in hot Austin, Texas, while providing an attractive, natural alternative to fencing, hedges or walls along sidewalk or street. By creating a low berm that feels right and natural, the Trimbles raised the height of their garden one to two feet. The planted berm screens the sidewalk and street from the entry garden and covered porch.

DESIGN PRINCIPLES

ﾍ *The front lawn has become a sacrosanct element of the American front garden. Find your level of comfort as you begin to reduce or remove that lawn.*

ﾍ *Lawn needs to be shaped, just as beds need to be shaped. The line of the front of your house can often generate the lines of your lawn.*

ﾍ *Putting in a bed, fence or hedge out by the street or sidewalk will not only make your front garden more private, but will also enable you to create a large, green, shaped lawn between those beds and the front of your house.*

ﾍ *Terracing a sloping front lawn with a low retaining wall will place your house on a more comfortable-looking, level plane that will read as an extension of the first floor of your house.*

ﾍ *Plant both sides of the walkway to your front door and then sweep that planting style across the whole front of your house. The resulting lawn panels will be large and dramatic and act as a coherent setting for your new gardens.*

Chapter 6
Gardens Out to the Sidewalk or Street

ONCE YOU GAIN CONFIDENCE developing the garden around your front door, you'll very likely want to make that garden bigger, either by running it all along the front of the house or by expanding outward into the front lawn. Or you might leap over a central lawn to develop a garden out by street or sidewalk. As time passes you may well decide to take up all the front lawn to garden the entire area between house and street. It's that garden from house to street that I want to address in this chapter. Before reading on, review figures 1.4, 2.6 and 3.5., and then look ahead to figures 7.3, 8.4, 8.5 and all the images on pages 125 to 136. Each of these photos, as well as the five in this chapter, will show you how people across America are removing all the lawn at the front of their homes and filling the resulting space with richly planted gardens.

A Ten-Foot-Wide Entrance Garden

To be in good proportion with the front of your house, the ideal entrance garden should be at least as deep as the front of the house is high, but sometimes that is simply not possible; figure 6.1 shows why, and what can be done to make that narrow space attractive.

First, the designer of this garden on Martha's Vineyard, off the coast of Massachusetts, has made the most of a shallow garden by giving it a firm vertical edge: a white picket fence in front of a white clapboard house. This fence provides an appropriate separation between public sidewalk and private house. The gate in this low fence further separates public from private while also enlarging the feeling of the space by giving guests an opportunity to swing the gate open, enter and then turn to close the gate.

Other details expand the feeling of space. Both the steps leading up to the landing, as well as the landing itself, are sufficiently wide—there is adequate room for two benches that are extensions of the fence and railing behind them. The color white also helps. It flows from the wall of the house down into the bench and railing and out to the picket fence.

The boxwood hedge strengthens the role of the fence in separating garden from sidewalk. The lily of the valley shrub (*Pieris japonica*) adds the one nonlinear shape in this elegant entry garden with its contrasting natural form, texture and height, one not controlled by obvious pruning. Furthermore, the white blooms visually tie this plant to all the white-painted surfaces in front of and behind it. To bring just a bit of color other than white and green to this elegant setting, the owners of The Charlotte Inn placed an informal wooden basket of daffodils and

FIGURE 6.1 *A traditional house on Martha's Vineyard, Massachusetts, is answered by a traditional garden in this very narrow space between house and sidewalk incorporating a white picket fence with gate, shorn boxwood hedges and lily of the valley shrubs* (Pieris japonica).

fragrant hyacinths on the right-hand bench to add detail and lightness.

Another element of this successful entry garden is its height. Had there been no fence, had the hedge been lower and the seven-foot-high pieris been replaced by a two-foot-high *Skimmia japonica*, the front of this house would have loomed overhead.

If you have even ten more feet between the front of your house and the sidewalk, you could replicate this design and then plant other evergreen and deciduous shrubs in the gap between the back of the hedge and the face of the pieris. Or you could not include the hedge, thereby giving you twelve feet of plantable space for something like *Rhododendron Weston's* 'Pink Diamond'. As the famous California-based landscape architect Thomas Church said, "The only limit to your garden is at the boundaries of your imagination."

A House within a Garden

Figure 6.1 implies New England restraint; figure 6.2 shows California exuberance and neighborliness. Here, the owners of two adjoining lots in Oakland have each developed what feels like a single garden that runs from house to sidewalk, with no lawn, just as Suzanne Porter and Ann Leyhe have done in figure 2.3. The California buckeye (*Aesculus californica*) underplanted with the ornamental grass *Stipa arundinacea* is part of the neighbor's garden. This garden, designed by owner Davis Feix, runs from the house in the background of this photo right out to sidewalk's edge.

FIGURE 6.2 *This entry garden near downtown Oakland, California, sets this house into a garden, one that is in full view from the sidewalk. The yellow-blooming succulent is* Sedum dendroideum; *next to it grows the gray-leaved* Senecio mandraliscae. *Both thrive near the California buckeye tree* (Aesculus californica). *Design by Davis Feix.*

FIGURE 6.3 *Rather than consult the house for the lines of her garden, Webber chose to plant the entire space between house and sidewalk with a collection of drought-tolerant plants that would not require irrigation. Path, structure and layout are subservient to her interest in tough plants suitable for her climate. Design by owner Nancy Webber, a landscape designer in Austin, Texas.*

He has combined all three levels of plants in this one garden: primary trees, secondary shrubs and tertiary perennials. While his interest clearly lies with succulent-leaved herbaceous plants, he has interspersed them among a mix of mounding and upright flowering shrubs, both deciduous and evergreen. Every plant contrasts in a pleasing way with its neighbor so their differences are clear. And because the house is painted light beige and the roofing material is only slightly darker, the house recedes into the background, allowing plants to take center stage.

There is one other point you need to keep in mind: this entry garden slopes away from the house down to the sidewalk. By planting higher shrubs near the house and lower shrubs and ground-hugging perennials in the foreground, it is clear the owners of this garden are interested in sharing their garden with passersby.

Plant for Your Climate, Your Zone

On pages 16 to 29, I wrote about how the style of your house can generate the style of your entry garden: cottage garden in front of a small, cozy cottage; a fenced herb garden in front of a two-hundred-year-old unpainted clapboard house in Massachusetts. Nancy Webber's home in Austin, Texas, could just as well be in New England, yet her garden is a drought-tolerant xeriscape (figure 6.3); in fact, she calls her garden design business Ground Xero.

FIGURE 6.4 *By installing a roughly four-foot-high wire fence a few feet back from the sidewalk and festooning it with Rosa 'Lady Banks', designer and owner David Yakish is able to separate his front garden and patio from this sidewalk in Sacramento, California.*

Webber gardened all the way from house to sidewalk with agaves and grasses, yuccas and cacti, flowering shrubs, perennials and bulbs that can adapt to the rigorous dry conditions of central Texas, made especially dry when a huge Post Oak fell in her front garden, exposing previously shaded plants to blazing sun. As you can see, she is honoring the plants from her region, and is not swayed by the architecture of her house. She is gardening exactly the way that pleases her, and she wants her neighbors and passersby to see what she's about and share in her enthusiasm for plants. There is no fence (and also no irrigation system to play a part in emptying the regional aquifers). Webber accepts climate and conditions and plants accordingly. Take a cue from Webber and plant a garden of plants native to your region in full view from the sidewalk.

Separating Sidewalk from Entry Garden

David Yakish, the designer and owner of this garden in Sacramento, California (figure 6.4), has gone in a very different direction from Webber. He likes his privacy, and you may well like yours too. In designing his garden, he put up a wire fence near the sidewalk so that he can garden in front of and behind it, then also installed a patio behind it. To further create separation between sidewalk and entry garden, he built a four-poster arbor over the garden entrance but offset them so that the upright posts do not frame a view of traffic going by from his front door. To draw attention to this offset entrance, he placed both his mailbox and its decorative metalwork near the entrance and then placed a hollowed-out, sculpted stone right next to it to create a reflecting basin to introduce a note of calm.

To form the rectilinear path from sidewalk to front door, one that broadens into a patio, Yakish used cast, tinted concrete that mimics tightly fitting stones. To lend a touch of authenticity to the concrete, he designed an inlay of eight cobbles to form a diamond that marks the center of the entry arbor. He then repeated the brick-red tint in the concrete path in the terra-cotta pots further inside the garden; materials used in this way help underpin unity and coherence.

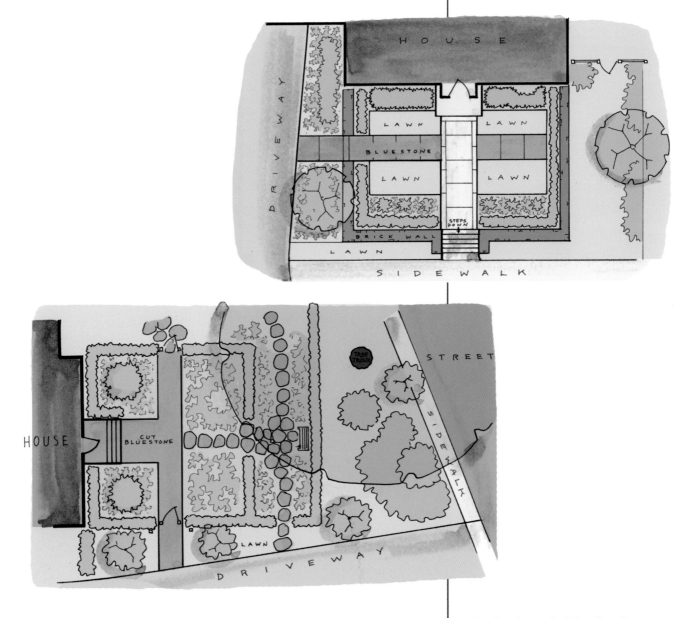

Bands of Garden, Bands of Lawn between House and Sidewalk

To make a small garden feel bigger, Japanese garden designers often run many horizontal bands of plants, paths and structures across the width of a garden, parallel with the nearby wall of the house. As you sit in or at the front of a house and look out over such a garden, your eye is stopped momentarily as it travels from foreground to background by each hedge, path or massed set of plants.

FIGURE 6.5 *The width and position of french doors running across the front of this house suggest the edges for the pool, lawn and other garden elements. The result is that the garden reads as an extension of the living room. Design by owner Wayne Renaud, Mississauga, Ontario.*

Wayne Renaud, who is a landscape architect in Mississauga, Ontario, Canada, did just the opposite (see figure 6.5). He ran a series of long, narrow garden elements *perpendicular* to the front wall of his house to emphasize the length and linearity of his entry garden. Look from left to right in this photograph and you will see several of the long, narrow lines: the fence covered with a vine; the garden between the fence and the narrow pool; the straight, bluestone walkway from the entry doorway to the house; the panel of lawn you can just see to the right of the photograph. By choosing to make his garden read as a series of elongated spaces, the outer ends of which are hedged off from the nearby street, Renaud created a totally coherent garden.

I bring this alternative up because you can take a cue from Renaud. Break up your front garden into separate long, narrow spaces that run perpendicular to your house rather than parallel with it, as you saw in figure 4.6. To help you find the right place for the edges of those long, narrow elements, look to figure 6.5 and you'll see the edges of Renaud's pool, bluestone walkway and lawn all line up with the edges of doors or pairs of doors. House and garden relate. No other photograph you will see in this book depicts a garden that is divided up in these long, narrow beds, so this photo is a particularly important alternative.

DESIGN PRINCIPLES

∽ *When you run a garden all the way from house to sidewalk, you need an overarching idea that will help you decide what to do and what not to do: a drought-tolerant xeriscape, a collection of succulent plants, an English cottage garden, an herb garden, or whatever style is right for you and your house.*

∽ *If the space between house and sidewalk is narrow, install a fence or hedge out by the sidewalk to enclose it as garden space. Choose plants that will grow at least to the bottom of your first-floor windows.*

∽ *Decide whether to screen off the garden from passersby or keep it open to their view.*

∽ *Consider joining with a neighbor to create a garden that runs across the area in front of two adjoining houses.*

Chapter 7
Creating Edges: Walls, Fences and Gates

FENCES AND WALLS help separate street from garden. They increase the sense of enclosure and privacy in your garden and can provide a background for a garden in front of or behind them. Gates through a wall or fence also increase that welcome feeling of entrance and transition—of leaving the sidewalk or driveway behind and entering a garden. Fences and walls help keep dogs and wandering children out of your garden. And because a fence can be solid or see-through and anywhere from three to even eight feet high, the degree of separation a fence can give you between house, garden and street is up to you.

There are a number of questions to answer as you decide whether or not to use a permanent built structure to separate street from garden. A built structure can appear more opaque, more permanent than plants. Many of the answers to these questions will go to the heart of your relationship with your neighbors and your own comfort level in being partially or wholly screened from the sidewalk.

Are there any municipal codes driving the dimensions or materials of fencing or walls at the front of your property?

Are there setback requirements that will determine how close to the sidewalk or street you can install a fence or wall?

If municipal codes allow for fences or walls, how will neighbors react to your fence or wall? Might it be a good idea to consult with them before proceeding?

Do you want the fence to simply separate your garden visually from the street or sidewalk, or do you want it to keep children and dogs out of your garden as well?

(FACING) FIGURE 7.1 *A simple white picket fence is just right in front of this unassuming blue house in Eugene, Oregon. There's nothing better than red tulips against a white fence.*

If you decide to go ahead with a fence, should it be see-through, as with pickets, and three to four feet high so passersby can look into your garden, or should it be opaque and six to seven feet high so you claim complete privacy from street and sidewalk?

If you decide to install a wall or fence that runs parallel with the front of your house, how far out should it be from the house?

What materials should the wall or fence be made of?

The Picket Fence

The picket fence is perhaps the most approachable fence you could build. As you can see in figures 7.1 and 7.2, the picket fence is a traditional, familiar structure when built in front of traditional, familiar homes. Because gaps between uprights allow light, air and plant foliage to flow through the fence, it is easily integrated with a garden in a way that walls and solid fences are not. Those gaps lighten the look.

The warmth and comfortable feeling of the picket fences in these two images come from different sources. The white picket fence on a street in figure 7.1 is made of broader pickets than those in figure 7.2, so it feels like more of a separator than the unpainted cedar pickets. The downward sweep of the white pickets between each of the fence posts reduces the visual mass of the fence while also making the pickets feel as if they were flexible and suspended from the posts. This detail makes the fence feel softer, more decorative.

FIGURE 7.2 *Owner Ann Marie Jensen worked with designer Andrew Grossman to create this fenced entry garden in front of her traditional home in southern Vermont. House, fence and garden all rise out of the same historical tradition.*

By setting the fence back two feet or so from the sidewalk, as you see in figure 7.1, the owners soften the look of the fence by planting in front of as well as behind it, thereby integrating fence and garden. The color white adds further integration; white paint is repeated in fence and chairs. The crab apple blooms white, as do the plants in the pot on the porch and the vine trained across the porch overhang. Even in front of this modest home, such a fence lifts the atmosphere of the garden.

The picket fence in figure 7.2 plays a very different role. Ann Marie Jensen, the owner who designed this garden with Andrew Grossman, lives in a rural area of southern Vermont. She already has privacy, so she doesn't need separation; she needs enclosure. Jensen uses this fence to create edges, to create a cozy surround for her entry garden. Certainly it separates her house from the nearby driveway as well, but that is not its major role.

There are some lessons to be learned from the position of this fence. If you want to install a fence off the front of your house but you don't want to put it all the way out by the street, measure the front wall of your house from ground level to the roof overhang and then flop that dimension down onto the ground. I suspect that's just what Jensen did when she built this fence outside her home. So, if the front wall of your house is sixteen feet high, set the fence at least sixteen feet out from the foundation. Then bring the side fencing back to some logical point on the house: a front corner, a setback that separates garage from front door, any architectural clue that will make the placement of fence feel right. Take a close look at Jensen's fence and how it meets the house at two logical points.

Once you have your fence logically situated, you can place a gate in it, as Jensen did, that can give rise to a straight path that runs parallel with or perpendicular to the front of the house. In Jensen's garden, both brick paths run through gates and lead to the front door. These logically situated paths divide her enclosed entry garden into the traditional four-quadrant entry garden. The result is a marriage of house and garden; a sharing of line, dimension and style; and the pleasing contrast between garden and architecture.

FIGURE 7.3 *Designer Linda Chisari worked with owner Debra Carl to develop the design for this enclosed entry garden in front of Carl's home in Cardiff-By-The-Sea in California. This opaque fence acts as a strong separator between garden and sidewalk.*

The house also answered Jensen's question about what material the fence should be made of. She looked at her unpainted cedar clapboard house and saw the wisdom of installing an unpainted cedar fence designed along traditional lines. Plant choice was simply an extension of all this thinking: a traditional garden of catmint and peonies, ferns and coralbells, daylilies and irises.

A Solid Fence or Wall

As you can see in figure 7.3, Debra Carl, the owner of this entry garden in California, installed a solid, opaque fence that neither light, air nor foliage can penetrate. In comparison with the two picket fences we've just looked at, this acts as a stronger separator between garden and sidewalk. This style of fence is more architectural than a picket fence and provides a uniform background for plants or garden ornaments placed against it. The picket fence, especially that in figure 7.2, is light, airy and semitransparent; this fence is solid, more assertive and a stronger presence in the garden.

That solidity is softened on the street side of the fence by setting it back two feet or so from the edge of the sidewalk. The resulting two-foot-wide planting bed then has a uniform background that clearly shows off the flowers, foliage and growth habit of flowering perennials planted in it. The same holds true for those plants set out between house and fence. When sitting in the house or standing at the front door looking out, the back of this fence acts as a uniform background for the entire entry garden while screening at least the lower half of automobiles as they pass by on the street. This screening is supported by the foliage of the tree ferns (*Cyathea*), and the taller trees set out to cool and contain this entry garden.

As you can see along the bottom of figure 7.3, Linda Chisari, the designer, has also planted the strip of ground between sidewalk and street, an area I cover on pages 120 to 129. By setting the solid fence about eighteen inches back from the sidewalk and planting that strip as well as the one between sidewalk and street, owner Debra Carl provides a long, narrow garden through which pedestrians walk. These long, narrow gardens also extend Carl's own garden just that much further, making her entry garden feel bigger.

In figure 7.4, you'll see virtually the same layout for an entry garden in Palo Alto, California. Of course, the plant selection is very different, but if you take a moment to compare figures 7.3 and 7.4, you'll see the designs of these two entry gardens have a lot in common, right down to the planted strip between sidewalk and street. One other point they have in common, one that you need to keep in mind when you consider a fence out by the street, is that both the wooden fence and the stucco wall read as an extension of the color and material of the houses themselves. Fence, wall and house act as bookends to contain the entry garden in a way that feels inevitable.

FIGURE **7.4** *This garden is planted with California natives. The tall tree to the right of the front door is* Sambucus mexicana. *The beige grass to the left in the image is* Festuca californica; Salvia clevelandii *fills the gap between sidewalk and wall.*

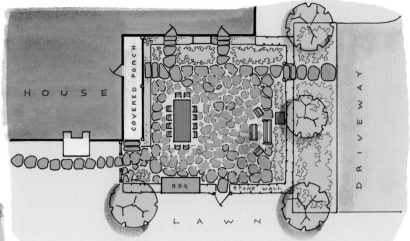

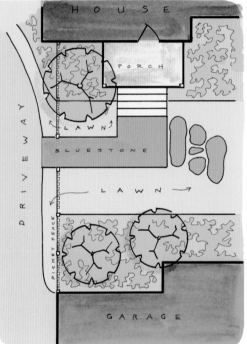

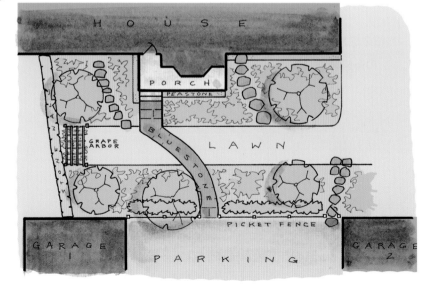

A Tall Fence, A Full Screen

In figure 7.5, you'll see a minimalist entry garden in front of a home in Lind, Oregon. While this garden echoes Japanese design elements, it helps you visualize what it might be like to totally screen off the sidewalk, street and even your own driveway from the many vantage points along the front of your house or within your entire front garden. One of the concerns many people have is that such a fence can look heavy, anonymous and unfriendly.

There are several details to study that will help you lighten the look of such a fence and entry arbor and give it a personality that standard stockade fencing cannot offer. First, look closely at the detail at the top of the fence in figure 7.5. The designer ran a rail along the

FIGURE 7.5 *Building a six- to eight-foot-high fence out by the street or sidewalk would enable you to utterly enclose your entry garden, as the owners of this home did in Lind, Oregon. Trees and shrubs planted on each side of such a fence keep it from feeling too imposing.*

top and then added a second top rail suspended by six-inch-high wooden spacers. The result is a lightness of spirit that would not have been evident had that top-most detail not been added.

Next is the nature of the entry arbor and the roof itself. It is held aloft by tall vertical posts that appear to be four-by-four-inch posts rather than a heavier-looking six-by-six-inch posts. Third, the lightness of the crosspieces atop the framework of the arbor adds an altogether airy, light feeling to this entire built structure.

The garden, minimalist as it is, further lightens the look. Birch trees with their light bark and wispy habit stand in front of and behind the fence. Boulders insinuate themselves into the pebble-embedded walkway and entry courtyard, thereby breaking down the edges of the concrete surfaces, linking garden to paving. The owners then planted both needled and broad-leaved evergreens to provide detail and year-round interest. This minimalist, low-maintenance entry garden, filtered through your own imagination, might well be a good model for you if you like a spare, restrained look in your garden.

Other Fencing Styles

Other styles of fence will create a different feeling in your garden.

ROUNDED OR SAWN SPLIT RAIL—*Rail fencing is appropriate for the front of homes in rural settings. It is informal, see-through, and brings with it associations of farmland and woodsy settings. Because split rail has a distinctive look, use it throughout your property as a unifying structure.*

ROUGH SPLIT RAIL—*This fencing, made by splitting eleven-foot-long black locust logs, is rougher than sawn or turned rails, and so belongs well away from the house. It would only be appropriate for an entry garden if it were used in front of a farmhouse, or any rustic home in the country.*

STONE WALLS—*These traditional walls bring with them a sense of history. They can be constructed with or without mortar—I far prefer the latter's look—along the front of the house, down the edge of a driveway, virtually anywhere. Run them parallel with the front of your house and they will*

*form a rectangular space between house and wall in which to create a tra-
ditional, mature entry garden around your new (or old) house. Stone walls
can also be topped with solid wooden fences to extend their height and
increase their ability to screen traffic and noise from your entry garden.*

To help you choose which fencing style is right for you, drive around
your neighborhood or region of the country to see what other people
have done with fences and walls. See what appeals to you, what doesn't
appeal, and then assess all your observations in light of your own
house and entry garden.

DESIGN PRINCIPLES

ॐ *Municipal codes often preclude or limit your choices regarding fences and walls out by the street. Check with authorities
before looking too far into fencing off your front garden.*

ॐ *Picket fences look good in front of traditional or small homes. Echo the style of the house in the design of the fence.*

ॐ *If you install a painted fence or wall out by the street, choose a paint color that echoes or matches that of your house.*

ॐ *Position a fence or wall out by the sidewalk two or three feet back from the sidewalk so that there is a planting space between
fence or wall and sidewalk.*

ॐ *If you want complete privacy, and municipal codes will allow it, install a six- to eight-foot-high fence at the perimeters of
your entry garden. Design it so it feels as light as possible.*

ॐ *Use gates to invite people in. Gates underpin the feelings gathered around leaving the public world of sidewalk and driveway
and entering a private garden.*

Chapter 8
Sitting Areas

SITTING IN A GARDEN is such an appealing idea. Sitting in a *front* garden is such a foreign idea. As we gardeners in North America hold tenaciously to the idea of planting evergreens along the foundation and then sweeping lawn from it down to the street, we give up any notion that setting out table and chairs at the front of the house is appropriate. But if we make a garden, if we enclose a space for living at the front of our homes, we then could actually *live* in our front garden and not just walk through our front yard on our way to the front door.

As you can see in figure 8.1, one way to live in your front garden is to sit on the front porch, and look out into that garden. Roberta and Scott Bolling, owners of McKenzie View, a bed and breakfast in Springfield, Oregon, where I once stayed, encourage their guests to sit on white wicker and cushions on their front porch and look out into a garden that separates driveway from house.

But let's say the front porch of your home looks out into a densely populated suburban area and onto traffic going by night and day. Go out and sit on your front porch, or, if you don't have one, take a chair and sit on the front lawn. Imagine how you could plant a few small trees several feet in from the sidewalk to claim your front lawn as a private space in which you could sit. Imagine interplanting those small trees with shrubs that would increase the feeling of privacy for a sitting area in your front garden. Let's look at a variety of ways that garden designers and homeowners have created sitting areas in their front gardens. One of them might spark your imagination.

(RIGHT) FIGURE 8.1 *The classic sitting area at the front of the house is the porch. By setting up an arbor for a clematis, by planting along the front of the porch as well as out by the driveway, you create a sense of enclosure and grace. Design by owners Scott and Roberta Bolling, Springfield, Oregon.*

Leave A Lot of Lawn

As you see in figure 8.2, the owners of this garden have created a sitting area in the ell at the front of their house in San Antonio, Texas. By expanding the brick walkway into a generous landing in the ell of their house, they were able to make room for a table and chairs. To enclose the immediate area around that small space, they planted a single boxwood in each of five terra-cotta planters and set them just far enough apart at the perimeter of the brick landing to allow for views into the garden. Because they wanted to leave a good deal of their front lawn in place, they only removed a strip of sod out by the street (out of view in the photo) to make room for small trees and shrubs that would screen traffic from view and make this sitting area feel private. To provide interest and color within this space, they planted small upright shrubs in pots on the brick and underplanted them with impatiens. They also hung a planted pot on the wall to provide detail and color to what would have been a featureless wall. This simple solution means that owners and their guests can actually sit in their front garden.

FIGURE 8.2 *Placing a sitting area in the ell of a house feels so right. By gathering a sense of enclosure at the perimeter of this sitting area as well as out by the road or driveway, the owners ensured a degree of privacy in this garden in Texas, even though a good deal of lawn remains.*

FIGURE 8.3 *Nancy Webber used the front wall of her house in Austin, Texas, as the backdrop for her shady sitting area. To provide a sense of enclosure, she installed a low retaining wall over which she could see into her extensive sunny front garden. The orange-flowering tree in the background provides pomegranates. Of this area, Webber says, "It's a nice shady place to sit, to greet guests and to linger saying good-bye."*

Create a Sitting Area along the Front Wall of Your House

If you look back at figure 6.3, you'll see Nancy Webber's garden at the front of her home in Austin, Texas. What you can't see in figure 6.3 is what you can see in figure 8.3: her sitting area along the front of her house. Because she planted a garden all the way out to the street, she wants to be able to sit in it. She wants to share her garden with passersby, but she also wants to claim a modicum of privacy for herself. By enclosing an area along the entire front of her house with a low stone wall and then paving the area between wall and house with mortared limestone, she made herself a sitting area in the spot in her front garden that is furthest from traffic and most private. Webber's plan might be a good model for you.

Now don't forget the rejoinder that I periodically return to in this book so as to keep you on track. Look at these images, manipulate them, change them in your mind so that the gardens in these photographs become an inspiration for your garden making. Look at both figures 6.3 and 8.3 and perhaps you'll say, "I don't want a garden that big, but I sure do like the idea of a sitting area right along the front of my house." Create that sitting area and then plant a garden that is only ten or fifteen feet wide in front of it. Then you can leave the remaining area of lawn between outer garden edge and street. Find your own comfort level with all these ideas; make them work for you.

FIGURE 8.4 *Ornamental grasses, daylilies, bee balm and other perennials combine with the crab apple to separate street and sidewalk from this sitting area off the front of a house in suburban Indiana.*

A Generous Sitting Area in a Small Front Garden

As you can see in figure 8.4, you don't need a deep front garden to make a sitting area. The Childress family lives in Indiana and worked with designer Anita Bracalente to turn what was a roughly thirty-five-foot-deep area of lawn between house and sidewalk into an engaging sitting area. This house, set in a suburban community, is close to the road so Bracalente separated street from sitting area with a crab apple tree underplanted with flowering perennials and ornamental grasses to enclose the space. She then looked to the house for cues as to what paving materials to use as a surface for the outdoor sitting area. The brick house gave her the idea to create a brick sitting area within the garden; the indigenous stone of the area gave her the idea to surround that brickwork with irregular pieces of Indiana limestone which, in turn, acted as the edge for the garden.

Now take a few moments with this picture to see what you could do differently to make this idea work for you:

>*If you want more privacy, plant more shrubs and fewer perennials out by the sidewalk. Would a fence rather than shrubs be more appropriate?*

>*If you are a shade-loving person, where might you plant a larger tree to provide shade? (Would three trees rather than one in figure 8.4 help you feel more enclosed yet not walled in?)*

>*What material indigenous to your area would you use for the sitting area, in addition to brick? What shape would you form with those materials?*

>*Would a gate be interesting to create more of a feeling of entering your sitting area?*

Now that you are near the end of this book, consider going back through the sections to see where you might place sitting areas in some of the gardens pictured. This exercise might well inform your decision as to where to place one in your own front garden.

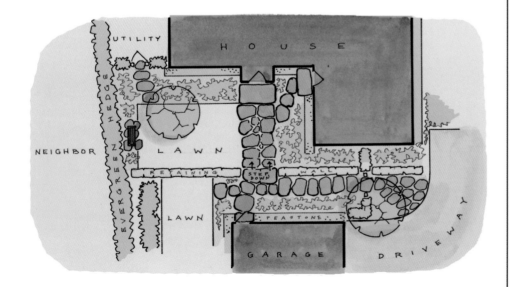

Sitting Out in the Garden

There is a big difference between Nancy Webber's entry garden and sitting area shown in figures 8.3 and 6.3 and the garden/sitting area designed by James Van Sweden in figure 8.5. By comparing them, you might see more clearly how to develop your own sitting area. Webber placed her sitting area adjacent to the house so it reads as an extension of the first floor of her house. Her sitting area lies in that space between house and garden and as such is associated equally with both.

When James Van Sweden designed this area for the Rifkinds on Long Island, New York, he set it ten feet or so away from the house, and under the branches of the large cherry tree. The result is that people are sitting within a garden rather than at its edge. There is a big emotional

difference between those two, and you need to determine which is more comfortable for you.

There is another major difference between Webber's whole front garden (figure 6.3) and Van Sweden's garden you see in figure 8.5. Van Sweden massed plants; Webber planted individual specimens. Where Webber has a single agave here and a single cactus there, Van Sweden has combined shrubs and perennials to create a calm, quiet, restful garden. Webber is celebrating the diversity of plants that can tolerate dry conditions; Van Sweden is massing plants to create a rich yet restrained interplay of contrasting colors, forms and textures. One is not better than the other; they're simply different approaches to garden design; you have to decide which would work best for you.

FIGURE 8.5 *James Van Sweden created a restful sitting area within a garden in which he massed plants that have different bloom and foliage qualities: an astilbe, a bamboo, an epimedium and the chartreuse-leaved ornamental grass* Hakonechloa macra 'Aureola', *among others.*

FIGURE 8.6 *Designer Marianne Faulkner created this entry garden/sitting area for clients in Charlotte, North Carolina, by broadening the walkway to the front door. She planted between the outer edge of this area and the nearby street to provide privacy.*

Broaden the Entry Path into a Sitting Area

Another way to make a sitting area in your front garden is to broaden the path from driveway to front door at some point along its length. As you can see in figure 8.6, designer Marianne Faulkner used stucco walls capped with bluestone to create an entrance into this garden space for her clients William and Robin Branstrom who live in Charlotte, North Carolina. By planting on each side of the entry to enclose this front garden, Faulkner made this area private and a world apart. Once the fieldstone path runs between the confines of the two stucco walls, it broadens into a sitting area. The bluestone cap to the stucco wall is about twenty-four inches above the surface of the walkway/sitting area and can double as a bench for larger groups.

DESIGN PRINCIPLES

❧ *If you have a front porch, sit on it and see how much traffic and noise is evident from where you sit. Consider where you might plant just trees, trees and associated shrubs or a whole garden to make your front porch feel more private.*

❧ *Consider setting a sitting area in the ell at the front of your house, or along the whole front of the house.*

❧ *Consider how you might design a sitting area that is separated from the nearby road with trees, shrubs and/or perennials to provide you with some degree of privacy.*

❧ *How could you broaden your entry walkway into a sitting area?*

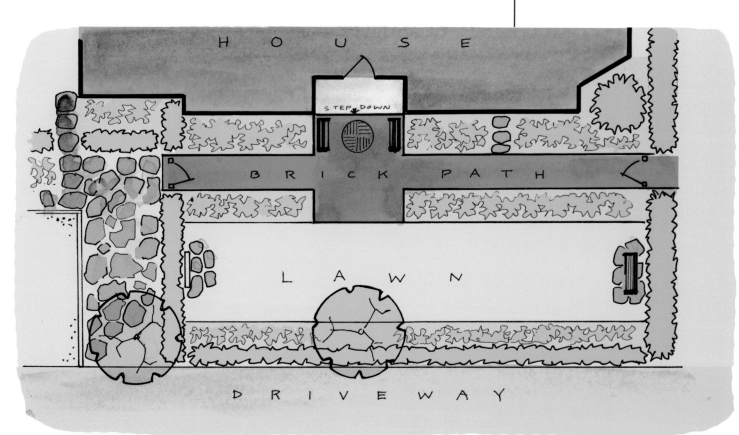

Chapter 9
The Strip between Sidewalk and Street

THE SPACE between sidewalk and street goes by many names across America: street-side garden, boulevard, tree lawn, curbside, parkway, parking or median strip, among many others. This area, which calls for low-maintenance, tough plants, is one that, along with the front garden in general, has been getting a lot of attention lately. A garden in this area is becoming an important extension of front gardens across America. By gardening this strip of normally neglected ground, you make your own garden feel bigger, you help screen both moving and parked cars when you're in your front garden, and you provide a richly planted garden for passersby to enjoy.

Todd Meier, the editor of *Fine Gardening Magazine*, where I am a contributing editor, has given me permission to reprint six Regional Reports that appeared in their September-October 2004 issue. Meier and his editors worked with six garden writers from six regions of America—the Northwest, Southwest, Mountain West, Upper Plains, Northeast and Southeast—to develop substantive information regarding how to garden in this challenging narrow strip. But before gardening this area, check with municipal authorities to see if there are any regulations in place that will have an impact on your design. After all, that strip of ground is typically not your property but that of the municipality in which you live.

Take other matters into account too: don't use plants that will flop and fall onto the sidewalk or street; don't use thorny plants or those that will block your view when pulling from your driveway into traffic.

(RIGHT) FIGURE 9.1 *Roses; the low, shade-tolerant evergreen Microbiotta decussata; hardy geraniums and sedums; purple-leaved plantain; red-pink-flowering agastache; and other perennials, shrubs and trees with purple foliage combine to make this median strip in Seattle, Washington, come alive.*

If you live in an area of the country where streets have to be plowed free of snow regularly or periodically, don't use any shrubs that will get damaged by that plowing. If your municipality uses salt to melt snow on the street, plant only salt-tolerant plants. And finally, the existing soil in that strip is likely to be infertile and compacted. Be prepared for some work to make the area amenable to gardening and limit the work to that possible with hand tools. If you get into deeper excavation with heavy equipment, you run the risk of hitting utility lines.

If you find that you are allowed to garden this area and you're prepared to take on the challenge, design the plantings so they feel like an extension of the garden at the front of your house. As you can see in figures 9.1 and 9.2, the designers of these California gardens repeat certain colors in both flower and foliage to the right and left of the sidewalk. (See also figures 4.2, 7.3 and 7.4.)

(LEFT) FIGURE 9.2 *This garden in a hot California climate is a cottage garden of lilies, chives, evening primroses, achilleas, lavenders and nicotianas. Combined with trees and shrubs, they provide a visual link down each side of this sidewalk in Danville, California. The owner/designer is Kristin Yanker-Hansen.*

DECORATING THE MAILBOX

Growing a vine or planting a shrub or group of perennials around the base of a mailbox certainly decorates the mailbox, but you have to be careful that it doesn't look too cute, too separate from the rest of your entry garden. If you can draw your mailbox into the whole fabric of your entry garden, as you can see in figure 6.4, do so. If your mailbox is freestanding, just a vine growing up its support will suffice.

(LEFT) FIGURE E *This Clematis × jackmanii cultivar flourishes on the mailbox and its post outisde a home in Pearce, Tennessee. Because most mailboxes are on the street, planting a vine on your mailbox can hint at the nature of your entry garden, including the colors people might expect as they enter it. Repeat that same vine inside the garden to add a note of coherence.*

Regional Guides

PROVEN PLANTS FOR BUSY ROADSIDES

Within a short walk to downtown shops, restaurants, offices and New York City transportation, my garden faces an urbanized, suburban street, a heavily traveled route in northeastern New Jersey. Plants in my street-side garden must tolerate clay soil, pollution, drying winds, pavement heat, road salt and hot afternoon sun. In addition, the plants are expected to thrive when packed into a tight space along the sidewalk and the street where constant pedestrian and vehicular traffic bombard the perimeter. Aesthetically, I strive to include plants that look equally as decorative from a speeding car as from my living room window. Is that a lot to ask from a plant? Not really. Here are some specimens that have proven to offer me beauty and brawn in this difficult environment.

—SUSAN VEELING *is a garden consultant and master gardener who applies her expertise to curbsides throughout Ho-Ho-Kus, New Jersey.*

10 Tough Street-Side Plants

1. ANNUAL SALVIAS (*Salvia splendens* cvs.) I grow annual salvias in the brightest red I can find. Planting them closer together than instructed, I feel they make the whole garden pop. They droop on only the hottest days and recover quickly with some water.

2. BLACK-EYED SUSANS (*Rudbeckia* spp. and cvs., USDA Hardiness Zones 3–9) The dark centers and vibrant petal colors of these plants are staples in my roadside garden. Resistant to parching and air pollution, they partner well with ornamental grasses.

3. DAYLILIES (*Hemerocallis* cvs., Z 3–10) Naturalized daylilies will tolerate drought and neglect while adding height and bold color to the mix. Multiplying freely, they grow well in and among boulders or at the base of a utility pole.

4. EULALIA GRASSES (*Miscanthus sinensis* and cvs., Z 4–9) The dense foliage of these grasses acts as a sound barrier, windbreak and natural fence. They adapt to most soils, and with slight support, they stand proudly in the heaviest of snows.

5. FEATHER REED GRASS (*Calamagrostis* x *acutiflora* 'Karl Foerster', Z 5–9) A strong, vertical element in my street-side garden, this showy grass grows beautifully in dry, poor soil and in the heat. 'Karl Foerster' flowers in June, well ahead of most other grasses.

6. FOUNTAIN GRASSES (*Pennisetum alopecuroides* and cvs., Z 6–9) Airy, mounding fountain grasses visually soften the hard edges of concrete. Salt and wind do not adversely affect them. These are superb plants to combine with spring bulbs.

7. NIPPON DAISY (*Nipponanthemum nipponicum*, Z 6–10) I plant the profuse-blooming Nippon daisy to rev up my autumn vignettes. This perky plant holds up well to sun, wind and less-than-perfect soil.

8. ORNAMENTAL ONIONS (*Allium* spp. and cvs., Z 4–10) Both *Allium giganteum* (Z 6–10) and the smaller *A. aflatunense* (Z 4–8) thrive in rocky soil and require little water and feeding. Their dried seed heads offer winter interest for a month or more.

9. SAGE (*Salvia* x *sylvestris* 'Blue Hill', Z 5–10) I plant 'Blue Hill' sage for its numerous, long-blooming sky-blue flowers. It requires little watering, and the occasional broken stem or damaged flower from passing traffic is not noticeable.

10. TULIPS (*Tulipa* spp. and cvs., Z 4–8) Heavy traffic discourages rodents, so I have had success with a variety of tulips. One or perhaps two saturated colors and a thick planting make a definite impact.

PLANTS WITH LONG-SEASON GOOD LOOKS

Snowplows and road salts are rarely an issue for gardeners in most of the South, but forget growing anything delicate, prized or fleeting at curbside. Pavement and passing cars make this a hot spot in an already hot environment. Water is often located at an inconvenient distance away. Road crews and utility companies occasionally exercise their right to make repairs. Not all passengers look before stepping out of cars. And, of course, dogs do what comes naturally during their daily constitutional.

To improve your odds for a successful curbside planting, start by amending the soil, which is probably compacted and of poor quality due to road or home construction. Provide passersby with solid landings on which to step, and avoid plants that snag stocking or that flop after it rains. Add a small patch of gravel, brick or stone for curbside recycling and trash pickup.

Most important, select tough plants with long-season good looks. After all, street-side plantings are in semipublic spaces where they are on view year-round. Close to the curb, use die-hard evergreen ground covers that seemingly thrive on abuse. Tuck in bulbs for splashes of seasonal color. Where there is room, select small shrubs or ornamental trees with flowers, berries, fall leaf color or evergreen foliage to increase year-round interest. Then look to reliable, long-blooming perennials to fill out the space. Also, think of your mailbox as a garden structure: drape it with small, flowering vines and plant a few annuals at its feet.

—LEE ANNE WHITE *is a garden designer and the photographer, author or editor of eleven books on landscape design.*

10 Tough Street-Side Plants

1. **AUTUMN FERN** (*Dryopteris erythrosora*, USDA Hardiness Zones 6–9) This evergreen fern will brighten shady curbs when the new, reddish foliage emerges each spring.

2. **BLACK-EYED SUSAN** (*Rudbeckia fulgida* var. *sullivantii* 'Goldsturm', Z 4–9) This easily grown, sun-loving perennial is quick to colonize but easy to control. It blooms for weeks each summer.

3. **BLACK MONDO GRASS** (*Ophiopogon planiscapus* 'Nigrescens', Z 6–10) A dense, clump-forming, evergreen ground cover with black foliage, this grass can withstand shade, some sun and trampling.

4. **BLANKET FLOWERS** (*Gaillardia* × *grandiflora* and cvs., Z 3–8) With deadheading, you'll enjoy these sunny red-and-yellow flowers from early summer through fall. It blooms the first year from seed.

5. **CLEMATIS** (*Clematis* 'Etoile Violette', Z 5–9) This wilt-resistant clematis has small purple petals with chartreuse stamens from May through August. It's lovely intertwined with a rose against a mailbox.

6. **GARDEN PHLOX** (*Phlox paniculata* 'David', Z 4–8) Masses of white flowers top 3- to 4-foot-tall stems from summer through fall. This mildew-resistant phlox takes full sun or partial shade.

7. **PINKS** (*Dianthus gratianopolitanus* and cvs., Z 3–8) This drought-tolerant, silvery carpet is blanketed with fragrant blossoms in spring.

8. **REBLOOMING DAYLILY** (*Hemerocallis* 'Happy Returns', Z 3–10) This petite daylily sports buttery yellow blossoms from May through the first frost.

9. **ROSE** (*Rosa* 'Ballerina', Z 5–9) Train three or four stems of this rose around a mailbox in opposite directions; it will don tiny pink blossoms all summer long. Pair it with a favorite clematis.

10. **WOODLAND PHLOX** (*Phlox divaricata*, Z 4–8) A reliable spring bloomer in light shade, it makes an excellent companion for spring bulbs and irises.

CHOOSE PLANTS THAT CAN
TAKE SALT AND TRAMPLING

The day I discovered several children in a flower bed in my front yard trying to overturn a boulder where a garter snake had taken refuge was the day I decided to put up a split-rail fence between that garden and the sidewalk. Faced with road salts, the careless tossing of litter, deposits from passing dogs, heat reflected off concrete or asphalt, plus the occasional stolen plant and stomping from the aforementioned snake hunters, street-side plantings can have a rough time of it. Gardens next to pavement are also difficult to irrigate. All too often, water runs off before it has a chance to soak in and this can result in a heavy fine in these times of drought.

Despite the challenges of growing a street-side garden, it's worth it because it can provide a transition between public and private spaces. Moreover, planting flowers where everyone can enjoy them is like giving your neighbors a bouquet of blooms every day.

Wise choices include resilient plants that tolerate drought and salt and that are common enough that their loss or destruction would not be devastating. Here are some that I recommend for this area; all thrive in full sun.

—MARCIA TATROE *tends her garden in Centennial, Colorado, and is the author of* Perennials for Dummies.

10 Tough Street-Side Plants

1. APACHE PLUME (*Fallugia paradoxa*, USDA Hardiness Zones 5–10) This shrub gets 2 to 8 feet wide. White, rose-like flowers bloom May to October alongside pink feather-duster seed heads.

2. CHEDDAR PINKS (*Dianthus gratianopolitanus* and cvs., Z 3–8) The flower color varies by cultivar, but all fill the air with a sweet, spicy fragrance in spring. They grow 6 inches tall and 12 inches wide.

3. RED-HOT POKERS (*Kniphofia uvaria* and cvs., Z 6–9) This perennial, with upright orange, yellow and red flowers in summer, grows 3 to 4 feet tall by 3 feet wide. Supplemental watering increases blooming.

4. RED VALERIAN (*Centranthus ruber*, Z 5–8) This perennial blooms all summer long (May through hard frost). This plant has reddish coral flowers and gets 2 feet tall. It likes full sun to partial shade.

5. SEA HOLLIES (*Eryngium planum* and cvs., Z 5–9) These steely blue thistle flowers, which bloom in summer, are both unusual and everlasting. The plant grows 30 inches tall and 24 inches wide.

6. SEA THRIFT (*Armeria maritima*, Z 3–9) This perennial, which grows 6 inches tall and 10 inches wide, has bright green tufts of foliage and pink flowers in spring.

7. SHADSCALE (*Atriplex confertifolia*, Z 4–10) The flowers are inconspicuous, but the yellowish or pinkish seed heads that follow are striking year-round. This shrub gets 2 to 3 feet tall and wide.

8. SIBERIAN SEA LAVENDER (*Limonium gmelinii*, Z 4–8) The lavender blue summer blooms stand up to wind and snow load to add texture to the winter garden. It grows to 30 inches tall and wide.

9. SULFUR FLOWERS (*Eriogonum umbellatum* and cvs., Z 4–8) This perennial grows 6 to 24 inches tall and 6 to 36 inches wide, and has bright yellow flowers in late spring to early summer.

10. WINTERFAT (*Ceratoides Ianata*, Z 3–10) Fluffy white seed heads in fall and winter are every bit as attractive as the white flowers in late spring. This shrub grows 30 inches tall and wide.

MIX PLANTS FOR A
LONG SEASON OF BLOOM

After struggling for years with the ugly brown grass on my boulevard strip, I decided to replace the turf grass with flower beds. The fall before I planted, I defined the beds with contractor's edging material. Then I placed several layers of black-print newspaper on the grass, layered mulched leaves and grass clippings over the newspapers, and sprinkled topsoil over the whole mixture. The beds were ready for planting the next spring and have thrived ever since. An annual layer of mulch keeps weeds down and helps to reduce the need for watering. To make the beds on my corner lot attractive from any angle, I grow taller plants in the middle with increasingly shorter plants up to the street and the sidewalk.

I've had a lot of success growing a variety of perennials and annuals, including spring and summer bulbs. My best-performing street-side plantings include plants that range from 3 inches tall to 3 feet high. All of the plants like full sun and are drought tolerant and long blooming. Except for the sweet alyssum, they also make great cut flowers. To prolong their blooms, I deadhead all but the dwarf Russian sage, sedum and sweet alyssum. My curbside plantings are always a work in progress and a great chance to get creative.

—THERESA STEHLY *teaches gardening classes through community education programs in Sioux Falls, South Dakota, and her garden has been featured on local television shows and garden tours.*

10 Tough Street-Side Plants

1. DUSTY MILLERS (*Senecio cineraria* and cvs., annual) With its deeply cut silvery leaves, this drought-tolerant bedding plant adds appealing texture. It grows 8 to 10 inches tall.

2. DWARF RUSSIAN SAGE (*Perovskia atriplicifolia* 'Little Spire', USDA Hardiness Zones 5–9) This plant is 2 to 3 feet tall with light blue flower spikes. The wispy blooms have an airy appearance.

3. MEALYCUP SAGE (*Salvia farinacea* 'Victoria', annual) This showy plant, with deep blue, ever-blooming spikes, works well in the front of a bed; it reaches a height of 16 to 18 inches.

4. OX EYE (*Heliopsis helianthoides* 'Summer Sun', Z 4–9) At a height of 3 feet with double yellow flowers, this plant is a great option for the middle of the border.

5. PURPLE CONEFLOWERS (*Echinacea purpurea* and cvs., Z 3–9) These 3-foot-tall plants have pinkish purple, daisy-like flowers, which attract butterflies.

6. 'PURPLE EMPEROR' SEDUM (*Sedum* 'Purple Emperor', Z 3–9) With reddish purple foliage and reddish flowers, this front-of-the-border plant (15 to 18 inches in height) is a nice change from *S.* 'Autumn Joy'.

7. SHORT GOLDENRODS (*Solidago* 'Baby Gold', *S.* 'Baby Sun', and *S.* 'Peter Pan', Z 5–9) These cultivars, 20 to 24 inches tall with bright yellow plumes, are more elegant than some of their wilder relatives.

8. SHORT MARIGOLDS (*Tagetes patula* cvs., annual) These tough, self-seeding plants add a durable touch of color. They reach a height of 8 to 10 inches, with blooms of bicolored yellow and bright orange.

9. SWEET ALYSSUMS (*Lobularia maritima* and cvs., annual) Let this elegant, 3- to 4-inch-tall self-seeder spill over the edge of a curb or sidewalk. It provides white, pink or purple honey-scented flowers all summer.

10. ZINNIA (*Zinnia elegans* 'Dreamland', annual) This little gem is resistant to mildew and has full-size flowers in an array of bright colors on a compact (10- to 12-inch-tall) plant.

CHOOSE PLANTS THAT LIKE LEAN SOIL

Eager to grow more plants, gardeners often look curb-side. The strip of land between sidewalk and street belongs to the city, but our gardening desires are met with encouragement by our municipality. Who can argue with the fact that flowers and small shrubs make the city look better than dead grass and weeds?

Unfortunately, a planting strip usually has some of the worst soil you've ever seen. It can be packed with clay or filled with a jumble of rocks, sand and silt. Compounding the problem is poor structure from being bulldozed, stockpiled, transferred and compacted.

Poor, lean soil is just what some plants prefer, so instead of amending the soil over a wide area, I choose plants that don't mind the tough conditions. Dragging the hose out to the edge of the street is unnecessary when I treat my planting strip like a tiny Mediterranean landscape by choosing plants that fit our similar, albeit cooler, climate: wet winters and dry summers. A good mulch goes a long way when it comes to suppressing weeds and moderating soil moisture in winter and summer. I sometimes use a layer of crushed rock instead of an organic mulch since many of these plants are used to living lean and mean.

Besides tough conditions, the biggest problem facing a street-side garden is visitors. Both people and dogs are accustomed to grassy planting strips, although for different reasons. People know it's fine to walk on grass but are unsure about a sea of lavender, so it helps to provide a path or two. People usually keep their dogs walking past planted street-side gardens (and on to someone else's grass); a garden seems to make them more aware of where they make their stops. It also helps that I am often out there, planting and puttering about.

—MARTY WINGATE *writes a weekly gardening column in the* Seattle Post-Intelligencer *and is the author of* Big Ideas for Northwest Small Gardens.

10 Tough Street-Side Plants

1. BEABERRIES (*Arctostaphylos × media* and cvs., USDA Hardiness Zones 7–9) These native shrubs have gray green leaves and cinnamon-colored bark, which are accented by pink heather-like blooms in spring.

2. BLUE OAT GRASSES (*Helictotrichon sempervirens* and cvs., Z 4–9) These evergreen grasses feature bluish leaves with fountain-like growth. They're easy to care for: just comb out their dead leaves in late winter.

3. CREEPING THYMES (*Thymus* spp. and cvs., Z 4–9) These fragrant plants love to grow over pavement. All they ask for is full sun, good drainage and a little housekeeping in late winter.

4. GLOBE THISTLES (*Echinops ritro* and cvs., Z 3–9) These perennials grow into impressive 3-foot-high stands. Cut the flowers and leaves back hard for a fresh flush of foliage that carries through autumn.

5. LAVENDERS (*Lavandula angustifolia* and cvs., Z 5–8) These plants are perfect for the feel of summer in Provence. After flowering, just barely cut the foliage back for a flush of new growth and a tidy look.

6. LEATHERLEAF SEDGES (*Carex buchananii* and cvs., Z 6–9) These outstanding evergreen grasses are around 2 feet tall and offer rusty red foliage, which blends nicely with neighboring perennials.

7. ORNAMENTAL ONIONS (*Allium giganteum*, Z 6–10, and *A. aflatunense*, Z 4–10) The blooms of these purple bulbous perennials appear in summer, then turn to ornamental seed heads as they fade.

8. PENSTEMONS (*Penstemon* spp. and cvs., Z 4–10) This group of shrubby evergreens has foxglove-shaped flowers on spiky stems in June and a second bloom if cut back after flowering.

9. ROCK ROSES (*Cistus* spp. and cvs., Z 8–10) Rock roses provide that quintessential Mediterranean look. They look best when left to their own, soft, mounding forms, not heavily sheared.

10. SUN ROSES (*Helianthemum* spp. and cvs. Z 6–8) These evergreen subshrubs bloom only once in late spring, but they offer excellent gray green foliage. Shear them after flowering for a tidier look.

LOW-MAINTENANCE PLANTS WORK BEST

In Southern California, where we garden 365 days a year, it's easy to get a little lazy because almost everything grows well with minimal tending. But I like to be strict with my plants; they have to work for at least nine months in my garden. Why waste great weather on a plant that doesn't seriously produce or, worse yet, dies back to the ground, leaving a bare spot? This is especially true of the parkway (the area between the sidewalk and the street), which serves as the visual entryway to your home all year round.

The soil in a parkway is often subsoil left from the building process and is virtually devoid of tilth and nutrients. So before you plant, prep the soil by adding organic materials such as worm castings or compost. My mantra has always been what my father used to tell me: rather than put a $50 plant in a 50¢ hole, put a 50¢ plant in a $50 hole.

In designing a parkway planting, I look for plants with certain qualities. Plants must be able to bounce back if stepped upon, rolled over or otherwise abused. Their flowers shouldn't encourage picking (unless you don't mind losing them). They must also be low maintenance, fragrant, butterfly- and hummingbird-friendly, and interesting year-round.

When putting plants that meet these criteria together, remember to create visual interest by combining plants that have long, narrow leaves with those that have more complex ones, or by placing bright yellow foliage against dark greens and reds. And remember to leave room for people to get in and out of their cars.

—LYNN MARIE HOOPINGARNER *is a master gardener in West Hollywood, California.*

10 Tough Street-Side Plants

1. **ANGELS' TRUMPETS** (*Brugmansia* spp. and cvs., USDA Hardiness Zone 11) This plant stops traffic with both its beauty and fragrance. A steady bloomer and fast grower, angels' trumpets can be trimmed to hold a standard tree-like shape.

2. **BEAR'S BREECHES** (*Acanthus mollis* 'Latifolius', Z 7–10) Another fast grower, this plant has beautiful dark leaves over a foot in diameter and amazing spikes of snapdragon-like flowers. It covers a large area but requires minimal maintenance.

3. **BUTTERFLY BUSHES** (*Buddleia davidii* and cvs., Z 5–9) Planted at the center of a parkway, butterfly bush can provide tall, drooping arches of color all summer long. A fast grower, it may require trimming to keep it in check.

4. **CORAL BELLS** (*Heuchera* spp. and cvs., Z 3–8) Coral bells form a low clump with thin, airy spikes of flowers that don't block the plants behind them. It also does not die back here as it does in colder regions. My new favorite cultivar is 'Amethyst Mist'.

5. **GRASSY-LEAVED SWEET FLAG** (*Acorus gramineus* 'Ogon', Z 10–11) Its floppy bright yellow and green leaves create year-round interest. A low-maintenance plant, it prefers to stay moist and tolerates the shade under trees. It performs best in zones that do not get excessively warm.

6. **LION'S EARS** (*Leonotis leonurus* and cvs., Z 10–11) The fuzzy bright orange blooms of lion's ear provide a great counterpoint in color, texture and shape to many of the sword-shaped leaves you might use as a border.

7. **NEW ZEALAND FLAX** (*Phormium* spp. and cvs., Z 9–10) This plant grows fast, tolerates poor conditions and requires little maintenance. The larger versions make good focal points, while the shorter cultivars are good protective borders.

8. **PIGSQUEAKS** (*Bergenia* spp. and cvs., Z 3–8) Shade lovers that work well under trees, these plants aren't as tough as others, so keep them away from foot traffic—and beware of snails and slugs.

9. **RED-HOT POKERS** (*Kniphofia* spp. and cvs. Z 5–9) Red-hot pokers need moisture to produce blooms, but the flowers are spectacular and long lasting. In addition, the leaves create an attractive vertical interest. A range of sizes and colors are available.

10. **WILD IRIS** (*Dietes grandiflora*, Z 9–11) Its height and leaf structure make it excellent for discouraging curious dogs. Beautiful, iris-like flowers adorn the plant nearly all year. Regularly pop off the seedpods to keep it blooming.

Chapter 10
Putting It all Together—
the Whole Front Garden

U P TO THIS POINT, I have been following a design process that addressed separate elements of an entry garden: the path itself, the garden around the front door, the uses to which walls and fences can be put, and all the rest. Now let's look at three whole entry gardens and how three different designers have pulled all these elements together into coherent front gardens. Two are in Oregon and one is on the coast of Connecticut, but it doesn't matter where these gardens are, nor does it matter what the houses look like. It's the useful principles that matter for you.

A Shady Entry Garden in Oregon

One of the first things you need to know when you begin to choose plants for your entry garden is which direction the front of your house faces and what the light conditions are. Some plants need sun, some need shade, and some tolerate varying degrees of each. Look at figure 10.1 and you'll see morning light coming from the east. The east is therefore to the right of the house, west is to the left, north is to the back, south is to the front. A south-facing house often means a sunny entry garden, but large Douglas firs and Oregon myrtle trees in this garden and on the street prevent much of that direct sunlight from getting to the ground. Here, a garden of shade-tolerant plants is a necessity if the garden is going to flourish. (See figures 10.2, 10.3 and 10.4).

When Sarah and Lance Robertson, the owners, asked designer Brad Strangeland for help with the design, they followed the same

FIGURE 10.1 *This is a makeover garden. Before there was only scraggly lawn and a few shrubs growing under the shade of mature Douglas firs. Rather than try to grow sun-loving lawn and perennials here, the owners accepted the shady conditions and created a flourishing shade garden. Design by Brad Strangeland for the Robertson family, Eugene, Oregon.*

sequence most designers follow, in fact, the same sequence I used to organize this book. First, they chose an overarching idea—a shady entrance garden with no lawn—in part because Sarah said, "The lawn that was there before seemed to be crying to be put out of its misery." While not all gardens under trees need to be informal, most are because that's the nature of woodland.

Once they selected shade and informality as their major variables, they designed the paths. There would be no straight lines in beds or paths. Curves would rule the day, not only because of their informality but also because paths could wander through this small space, giving a feeling of greater size.

The designer began by laying out the curvilinear paths, not concerning himself yet with what the material would be. The main path

FIGURE 10.2 *The plant list here is a classic one for shade gardens: rhododendrons, hellebores, hostas and ferns, heucheras, variegated Solomon's Seal and the fall-blooming anemone, among many others.*

from sidewalk to front door would be wider than the secondary paths that ran from the main path into various parts of the front garden. Those paths enabled him to break the big front yard down into smaller, more manageable parts; they would allow Robertson to explore her garden following different routes to different areas, one of which included a bench (figure 10.4) not ten feet from the street where she can sit in relative seclusion looking back at her house.

Once the paths were laid out, Robertson and her designer then chose brick-like pressed concrete pavers as the material for the paths. Look closely at figures 10.1 and 10.2 and you'll see that Strangeland marked both the beginning of the primary path and the junction of primary and secondary paths with a circular motif in the pavers. You'll also notice in figure 10.3 that the path curves around the trunk of a mature tree that already existed in the garden. All good curves in paths (and beds) have logic. There is always an answer to the question, "Why does that path curve there?"

To emphasize the link between front garden and those down the left (or west) side of Robertson's house, the designer set a white-painted arbor as a way to mark the entrance to the path into that side garden. Notice there are no fences, no walls, no structures other than the white arbor in the garden.

Once path layout was established and the material for it chosen, the designer turned to

FIGURE 10.3 *Variegated plants in a shady garden bring yellows and whites into an otherwise green garden. Variegation is carried in the leaves of a cutleaf maple; hostas, and the low, white-edged foliage of Hebe elliptica 'Variegata'.*

plant choice. You can see in all four photos of this entry garden that Strangeland planted larger shrubs along the east and west sides as well as along the front porch, but kept shrubs and plants lower by the sidewalk so that passersby could look into the garden. Once the major shrubs were located on the plan, the designer turned to minor shrubs and perennials. Look at figures 10.2 and 10.3 and you'll see how paths help determine plant choice: low plants are set on each side of the path and plants get taller as you move away from the paths.

Flowering broad-leaved evergreens, such as shade-loving rhododendrons, throw dramatic red flowers, a color that Robertson picked up in the planted hanging baskets on the porch. Variegated hostas and cut-leaf maples add touches of chartreuse and white throughout the entire growing season. Evergreens form the backbone of a garden in winter.

FIGURE 10.4 *Tertiary side paths of small stepping-stones link primary and secondary paths made of fitted pavers to provide access into the beds for maintenance. This side path also leads to the one bench in the garden.*

Wanting to sit in the garden (as well as on the porch overlooking the garden), Robertson placed a teak bench in the far corner of her entry garden where she can sit and look back to the house across the full depth and width of her garden. She placed the bench at the place in the garden that had the best view into it.

Now, please remember that the decisions—every element of the design sequence I've just walked you through—were all based on personal choices made by designer and owner. Their style might not be yours. Perhaps you would like a different material for your curvy paths. Maybe your front garden is in full sun so you can have a bit of lawn in the midst of your entry garden. Maybe you don't want a white arbor to lead guests into your side garden. But what you do gain from this sequence is just that—a sequence, an order of decision-making that you can follow. Let's look at another, very different, example.

A Sunny Front Garden

Unlike the shady garden we just looked at, this garden on the coast of Connecticut is in full sun the entire day (figures 10.5 through 10.7). At the very least, the fact that this garden is in full sun helped the designer, Nancy DuBrule, and her deeply involved client rule out all plants that require partial or full shade. Other than that, anything was possible. They first set out some of the goals for this entry garden:

> *To give screening from the road to gain more privacy, especially during the summer when traffic on the nearby coastline road is at its peak.*

> *To allow a profusion of summer-blooming flowering perennials and shrubs but no trees that would shade them.*

> *To have a vegetable and herb garden close to the kitchen.*

> *To create separation between driveway and garden.*

> *To be an informal, unselfconscious natural look that would greet guests as they walked down the length of this varied garden to the front door.*

> *To be an organic garden: no chemicals, please.*

(FACING) FIGURE 10.5 *The planted berm to the lower right in this photo screens the street and parked cars from the garden and supports a rich profusion of perennials and shrubs, one of which, Rosa 'Meidiland Scarlet', is in the foreground.*

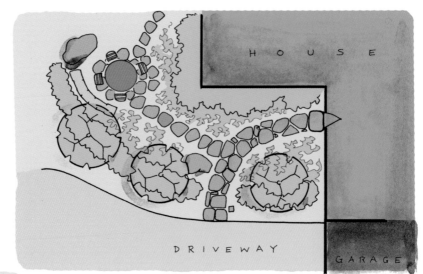

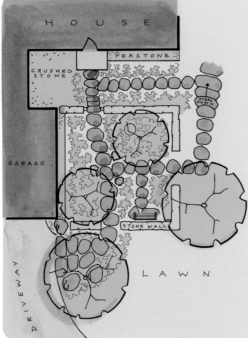

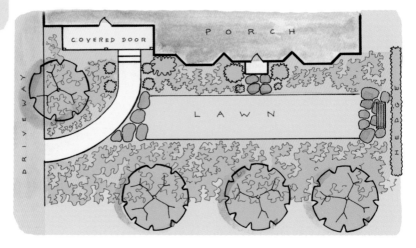

In setting up the broad layout for this garden, DuBrule started from the edges and worked in. She first designed two different fences to contain the garden along both sides and establish clear edges and a background for the garden. The white-painted fence you see in figure 10.6, which picks up the white-painted trim on the house, is solid, about four feet high and separates the garden from the nearby neighbor while also acting as a backdrop for flowering perennials inside the garden. She then chose a slightly lower white-painted picket fence for the other side of the garden close to the street (figure 10.7). By keeping it at around three feet high, passersby could look into the garden.

FIGURE 10.6 *As family or guests stand at the downstairs or upstairs windows, or on the covered porch looking into this garden, they have the feeling that they are in it. The fact that the garden is organic adds another level of pleasure to the experience. Design by Nancy DuBrule, Connecticut.*

Next she addressed the far end of the garden furthest away from the house where the shoreline road met the front of their client's property. Because the goal was to totally screen off the road and cars when looking out the first-floor windows of the house, or when in the garden, a six- to eight-foot-high fence would have been necessary, but that just felt too high, too imposing. She chose instead to build up a natural-looking topsoil berm where roses and perennials would provide a dune-like barrier between street and inner garden. Its far end, as you can see in figure 10.5, would also hide cars in the parking area out by the road. Furthermore, by making a three- to four-foot-high berm, a dimension in keeping with the two fences, out of rich water-retaining topsoil, DuBrule could plant flowering shrubs and perennials in the easily worked soil. Once the three outer edges of the garden were established, the designer ran a path that would lead family and guests from the parking area at the far end of the berm through the garden and up the steps to the screened front door.

Taking a cue from a traditional four-quadrant herb/vegetable garden so common in old New England gardens, she and her client developed the idea of four rectangular beds with pea stone paths running around all sides and among the four geometric beds. By aligning the central path with the center of the kitchen window (figure 10.6), DuBrule set up a relationship between house and garden.

Then taking a cue from the profusion of flowering perennials and shrubs planned for the front berm, she wrapped this same style of gardening around all sides of the central four-quadrant garden. The structured rectilinear garden set within a matrix of straight pea stone paths lies in happy contrast to a profusion of flowering shrubs and perennials all around it.

Once all decisions had been made about herbs, vegetables and flowering plants, the owner looked to furniture and ornaments. As you see in figure 10.6, she installed planted window boxes to soften the look of that broad expanse of wall in full view from the bench. In figure 10.7, she marked the center of the four-quadrant garden with a pedestal on which sits an armillary sphere. By pointing the arrow that runs diagonally through the metal bands to the North Star, the family can tell the time. DuBrule then set a bench at the far end of the herb-and-vegetable garden in full view from the porch and windows along the front of the house so that it would act as an invitation to come out of the house and sit in the sunny garden, one that provides food for the table, cut flowers for vases, and color and fragrance to sit within.

(LEFT) FIGURE 10.7 *This productive, beautiful and unself-conscious garden lies only a few feet from a nearby street, yet the fence and the inviting style of the garden makes it feel a world apart.*

An Entry Garden to Share

I am closing the book with this garden, in part because it bespeaks such a regard for others, such a sense of community. We plant gardens for ourselves, of course, but in doing so we plant them for others to enjoy as well. Richard Null is a biology teacher; Phyllis, his wife, is an artist. The Nulls live in a suburb of Eugene, Oregon, and over the years they have created this dazzling entry garden you see in figures 10.8 through 10.11. But their love of gardening doesn't stop there. This garden not only wraps all around their house, but it also runs up and down both sides of their block. Working with neighbors, they have planted shrubs and perennials up one side of the block and down the other. They have created what amounts to a community garden with special interest in April and May. Photographer Robin Cushman told me that the Nulls' garden "has stopped traffic in the spring. Phyllis plants grass in baskets and places them, with Easter eggs, all around the garden and even within reach of the sidewalk. Mother's Day is another time when folks from all over Eugene drive by."

Looking closely at figure 10.8, you'll see the Nulls' house below the level of the sidewalk. Look at 10.9, where photographer Robin Cushman was standing on the Nulls' parking spot, and you can clearly see how the garden relates to the neighbors'. Lawn is banished. In its place is a semi-shade-tolerant garden that blooms profusely in the spring as well as at other times of the growing season in this temperate Oregon climate.

FIGURE 10.8 *The Nulls have given lavish attention to their spring garden in Eugene, Oregon. A flowering Mt. Fuji cherry* (Prunus serrulata *'Shirotae') drops its pink-white petals on Darwin tulips, forget-me-nots* (Myosotis sylvatica), *candytuft* (Iberis sempervirens), *Rock Cress* (Aubretia deltoidea *'Purple Cascade'),* Ajuga reptans *'Bronze Beauty', and Azalea 'Hino Crimson', among many others.*

To quietly separate garden and house from the nearby street, the Nulls built up a soil berm along the edge of the sidewalk and strengthened it with bits of retaining wall and boulders along the path edge (figure 10.10). They also used boulders and rock set into rather than on this soil to retain the soil (see figure 10.11) and to provide planting pockets for azaleas; variegated-leaved dogwoods; large ferns; and no end of perennials, ground covers and bulbs to bring this space alive. They planted the flowering Mt. Fuji cherry (*Prunus serrulata* 'Shirotae') to provide mass, shade and that remarkable profusion of bloom you see in figure 10.8. They then linked the landing by the front door to a simple crushed-gravel path that provides access from the front and down the side to the back gardens.

FIGURE 10.10 *This gravel path runs from the parking/entry area by the front-door landing and roughly parallel with the street before turning left to lead into the side and back gardens.*

THE DESIGN SEQUENCE

1. *Write down the requirements you have for your front garden. The list could include a sitting area, a vegetable or flower garden, screening from the street—that is, all the elements of an entry garden I have been writing about, tailor-made to your requirements.*

2. *Measure the front of your house and the entire potential garden space. Include the edges of your property as it abuts your two neighbors and the street or sidewalk.*

3. *Assess what's already there that will drive your design—sun or shade; sloping or flat ground; dry or moist soil; in an urban, suburban or rural setting—and then choose a style, an overarching idea, that will help you know what to do and what not to do.*

4. *Assess the nature of the front of your house including its height and width, its materials, its color, and the position of the front door and windows.*

5. *Assess the relationship between your front door and the driveway to help you determine where the path will go between the two.*

6. *Use the path to divide the large space into two or more smaller parts that can be more manageably designed.*

7. *Decide whether or not you want to create a sitting area in your front garden.*

8. *Once you have the layout established, choose plants by proceeding from the biggest to the smallest—trees first, then shrubs, then perennials, ground covers and bulbs.*

9. *Select garden furniture in accord with the style of your house and garden and then set the chairs, tables or benches in the garden so they take advantage of your best views.*

10. *Choose pots in light of the colors of your house or the dominant colors in your garden. Plant them with annuals and perhaps even perennials or small shrubs to reflect the mood and nature of your garden. Set the pots relative to paths, steps and furniture.*

11. *Choose a few garden ornaments that have personal associations. Use them sparingly. An overdecorated, busy-looking garden is not restful. Lay out the ornaments to mark key points in your garden such as the junction of paths, the entrance to a path, or near the beginning and end of a straight path.*

12. *Invite your neighbors over.*

FIGURE 10.11 *The soil berm allowed the Nulls to separate sidewalk and nearby street from this part of the garden planted with* affodils (Narcissus *'Pink Charm'),* Darwin hybrid tulips, Corydalis flexuosa *'Blue Panda',* Pulmonaria rubra *'Red Start',* pimedium versicolor *'Sulphureum',* Maidenhair fern (Adiantum pedatum) *and* Sword Fern (Polystichum munitum).

Afterword

Learn by Comparing the Content of Photos

Now that you have been through the whole book, you probably feel ready to begin the design for your own entry garden. As you do, you may well run up against certain parts of the design that you find difficult to think through. For example, if you're not sure *where to plant spring-flowering bulbs in your entry garden,* refer back to figures 5.6, 6.1, 7.1, and 10.8 through 10.11. You'll learn a great deal about where tulips and daffodils can be set and how to combine them with other plants.

If you aren't sure *what materials to use to make an entry path* from the driveway to the front door, go back through every photo and look just at the materials paths are made of. If you're not sure *if you want a curving path or a straight path,* look back at photos, paying attention only to the shapes of paths but don't pay attention to the materials they're made of, or anything else in the photo for that matter. If you're thinking about *how to handle the beginning or end of a path,* look just at photos that show those areas of entry paths.

Here are some other categories you could review in the photos in this book—and other garden design books and magazines you have—for ideas:

- *Furniture and its placement*
- *Lighting along garden paths and on front porches or by doors*
- *Front-door landings and their materials*
- *The choice of materials for your paths and their colors relative to the colors and materials of your house*
- *Paint colors in both house and garden structures*
- *How steps to house or porch are handled*
- *How trees are used*
- *How shrubs and large-scale perennials such as ornamental grasses are used in entry gardens*
- *How smaller perennials and ground covers are used*
- *How boulders are set into an entry garden*
- *How gardens are set into the ell of a house*
- *How to plant just outside your front windows*

By comparing and contrasting specific elements within the photographs in this book, as well as those in other garden design books, you can create your own welcoming garden.